Mr. Maurice Knows It All
... and tells you so

James M. Flammang

TK Press
a division of Tirekicking Today (est. 1993)
Des Plaines, IL, USA

Mr. Maurice Knows It All ... and tells you so

Copyright © 2014 by James M. Flammang

Copyright registered: May 2015

Second Printing: June 2016

All rights reserved.
No part of this book may be used or reproduced in any manner whatsoever without written permission, except in the case of brief quotations embodied in critical articles and reviews.

Print edition published by TK Press (a division of Tirekicking Today), Des Plaines, IL 60018

ISBN: 978-0-9911263-3-0

Cover design and photos by James M. Flammang

For Louise, who discovered Mr. Maurice — created by two older ladies — at a London festival. And for Marianne, who recognized his magnificence at first glance.

Contents

Introduction ix
1. Mr. Maurice and Work 1
2. Mr. Maurice and Ambition 3
3. Mr. Maurice and Money 5
4. Mr. Maurice and TV 7
5. Mr. Maurice and Movies 9
6. Mr. Maurice and the Opposite (Sex) 10
7. Mr. Maurice and Knowledge 11
8. Mr. Maurice and Misbehavior 13
9. Mr. Maurice and Dignity 14
10. Mr. Maurice and Guilt 16
11. Mr. Maurice and Politics 17
12. Mr. Maurice and Inequality 19
13. Mr. Maurice and Citizenship 20
14. Mr. Maurice and Luxury 21
15. Mr. Maurice and Opinions 22
16. Mr. Maurice and Empathy 24
17. Mr. Maurice and Secrecy 25
18. Mr. Maurice and Waste 27
19. Mr. Maurice and Communication 28
20. Mr. Maurice and Fine Dining 30
21. Mr. Maurice and Humans 32
22. Mr. Maurice and Daily Life 34
23. Mr. Maurice and Family Life 35
24. Mr. Maurice and Gambling 36

25. Mr. Maurice and Consumption 38
26. Mr. Maurice and Status 39
27. Mr. Maurice and Groups 40
28. Mr. Maurice and Transportation 41
29. Mr. Maurice and Games 43
30. Mr. Maurice and Science 45
31. Mr. Maurice and History 47
32. Mr. Maurice and Religion 48
33. Mr. Maurice and Vanity 50
34. Mr. Maurice and Social Media 51
35. Mr. Maurice and Technology 52
36. Mr. Maurice and Fun 54
37. Mr. Maurice and Relaxation 55
38. Mr. Maurice and His Inferiors 56
39. Mr. Maurice and Immigration 57
40. Mr. Maurice and Illness 58
41. Mr. Maurice and War 59
42. Mr. Maurice and Sports 62
43. Mr. Maurice and Education 64
44. Mr. Maurice and Telephones 66
45. Mr. Maurice and Advertising 68
46. Mr. Maurice and the Law 69
47. Mr. Maurice and Violence 71
48. Mr. Maurice and Traffic 72
49. Mr. Maurice and Patience 74
50. Mr. Maurice and Conformity 75
51. Mr. Maurice and Interactivity 77
52. Mr. Maurice and Privacy 79
53. Mr. Maurice and Discrimination 80

54. Mr. Maurice and Travel 82
55. Mr. Maurice and Cleanliness 84
56. Mr. Maurice and Ownership 85
57. Mr. Maurice and Pests 86
58. Mr. Maurice and Charm 87
59. Mr. Maurice and Bad Behavior 89
60. Mr. Maurice and Generosity 90
61. Mr. Maurice and Courtesy 92
62. Mr. Maurice and Ethics 93
63. Mr. Maurice and Trust 94
64. Mr. Maurice and Time 95
65. Mr. Maurice and Fashion 96
66. Mr. Maurice and "isms" 98
67. Mr. Maurice and Security 99
68. Mr. Maurice and the Occupiers 101
69. Mr. Maurice and Business 102
70. Mr. Maurice and Salesmanship 104
71. Mr. Maurice and Slimness 106
72. Mr. Maurice and Food 108
73. Mr. Maurice and Alcohol 109
74. Mr. Maurice and Languages 111
75. Mr. Maurice and Worry 112
76. Mr. Maurice and the Wild Life 113
77. Mr. Maurice and the Past 115
78. Mr. Maurice and the Future 116
About Mr. Maurice 118
About the Author 119

Introduction

I first met Mr. Maurice when he was a youngster, arriving on U.S. shores with the eagerness of any first-time visitor. Actually, he was already 25 years old – and is still 25 years old.

In fact, he intends to *always* be 25. After all, he often says, if you determine that 25 is the ideal age, why would you not make yourself exactly that for your entire existence on earth?

Mr. Maurice does have one distinct advantage in that respect. He is not, in the usual sense of the word, alive. This is a matter of some delicacy. To his many friends and even greater circle of admirers, Mr. Maurice is far more alive than many – perhaps most – humans of their acquaintance.

So, *who* is Mr. Maurice? A mere glance at his photo reveals Mr. Maurice's French heritage, but he was actually born – or more precisely, knitted – in London, England. He came to the U.S. as a gift, to a married couple who had long been drawn to pigs of every persuasion.

How could they resist that soft, rosy-tinged pelt, that jaunty beret, the boldly-striped pullover shirt that lends an air of mysterious deeds, that elegantly-shaped tail. This was clearly a pig among pigs, as it were.

Little time passed before it became evident that Maurice – so named by his British creators – was no ordinary pig, stuffed or otherwise. Soon, he began to talk.

Mr. Maurice Knows It All ... and tells you so

And talk, and talk. There seemed no end to his opinions on virtually any topic.

Soon, too, it was obvious that Maurice's perspectives and explanations were invariably correct and on-target. Again and again, his penetrating intellect, his pointed wit, proved to be unmatched in either the porcine or human world.

Maurice himself eventually requested the "Mr." prefix, to better convey the dignity and value of his many assertions. He pondered other titles: professor, doctor, potentate. But he rejected each as being excessive. Despite his incredible intelligence and philosophical excellence, not to mention his total self-absorption, he is underneath it all a modest pig.

Mr. Maurice rules his piggie family with an iron hoof. He prefers that designation for his four appendages, over the crass-sounding "trotters," which implies an expenditure of effort. Mr. Maurice is not one to toil needlessly – if at all – as we shall see in these pages.

This book began several years before its actual publication, and Mr. Maurice has not been happy about the delay in getting his thoughts into print. In fact, he has threatened the author repeatedly, suggesting punishments too gruesome and humiliating to be mentioned in these pages.

All along, Mr. Maurice has envisioned his countenance upon the front cover, in all its brash pinkishness. Furthermore, he has envisioned absolute zillions of readers dashing down to their nearest bookstores, or filling out online order forms, to obtain one of the very first copies. At full retail price, of course.

Mr. Maurice Knows It All ... and tells you so

As we shall see later on, despite his many virtues, Mr. Maurice is one greedy little pig.

Here, then, are Mr. Maurice's perfect perspectives on many of the issues and events of our time, from personal to global and beyond. This is a work in progress, however. Mr. Maurice is always thinking, always looking ahead. We stand ready to pass along even more of his profound observations as they emerge.

James M. Flammang
Elk Grove Village, Illinois

1

Mr. Maurice and Work

Nothing explains Mr. Maurice more emphatically than his attitude toward toil. He favors it, to be sure – provided that someone else is actually *doing* it. While in his usual state of repose, Maurice often refers to the words of Mark Twain, who recalled that he could easily spend an entire day watching someone else work.

Maurice also loves to quote the legendary attorney Clarence Darrow, who declared: "I have always been a friend to the working man. I'd rather be his friend than be him."

This point must be made clear right off the bat: Mr. Maurice does not personally care to work. He loves to reap the benefits of *other* pigs' toil, of course. Human efforts, too. But he does not wish to raise a hoof in pursuit of physical labor himself.

His reluctance – indeed, abhorrence – is due in part to his distaste for perspiration. Mr. Maurice does not sweat. Ever. In fact, his favorite motto is: No Sweat. Therefore, he is not about to engage in any undertaking that could conceivably produce such a distressing result.

Mr. Maurice spends his days in a comfortable position, tended to by his family of piggies. Any toil that needs to be undertaken is assigned to a "lesser" pig: most notably, his avid lieutenant, Little Guy, known affectionately by pigs and humans alike as LG.

Whenever a trip needs to be taken, a plan developed, a crucial decision made, LG is called upon and comes to immediate attention, ready for action.

Naturally, Mr. Maurice cannot be bothered by any of these pesky details of daily life, many of which come perilously close to qualifying as work. The very thought of being close to such toil often makes Mr. Maurice's eyes twitch, his ear go on alert.

His beret may even slide down a bit, if he gets the sudden notion that someone might possibly call upon him – himself – to do something. At that point, he's sure to emit a few distressed oinks of anguish before leaning back in his regular spot, waiting for the danger of imminent work to pass.

Naturally, Mr. Maurice cannot risk any deleterious impact upon his legendary brain, caused by an excess of effort. Even though the quantity (and quality) of his brain cells exceeds that of any other creature known to mankind or pigkind, he would prefer not to take a chance on losing the effectiveness of even one of those teeny cells.

From Mr. Maurice's perspective, perhaps actor James Garner said it best in the western film *Support Your Local Gunfighter*: "I don't like work. It tires me out."

Truer words could hardly be spoken, in Mr. M's view.

□

2

Mr. Maurice and Ambition

Surprisingly, in view of his magnificence, Mr. Maurice is not an ambitious pig. Not for himself, at any rate. Mr. Maurice would like very much to see *you* get ahead – provided he stands to benefit in some small way. Or better yet, a *big* way.

If you're embarking upon a new career, or a new project, Mr. Maurice will be full of confident enthusiasm for your efforts. He will applaud you (provided the clapping is not too physically taxing, of course). He will cheer you on – while being careful not to strain himself.

You will note, however, that he does all this grandstanding from a comfortably seated position. No matter how much he likes you, and how strongly he backs your efforts, he is not about to exert himself on your behalf.

In other words, he has plenty of ambition for his human housemates; but none for himself. After all, there is no reputation to be earned, nor honors gained, when you're already at the pinnacle of it all.

He is, as we are observing, the potentate of all he surveys, the supreme leader of his piggie flock, admired and revered by pigs and people alike, all over the world.

He would like to be able to say he's admired all over the *universe* as well, but has not yet established whether there are any creatures out in the cosmos at all, much less those who would praise and laud him. Naturally, if there turn out to be such creatures, he is convinced that they, too, will fall under his spell, heeding the magnetism of his words (translatable even into languages as yet unheard on earth). No doubt, they, too, would be mesmerized – transfixed by the stellar beauty of his presence, the aura of magnificence that is irresistible to all.

As a result, Mr. Maurice does not hesitate to claim a compelling desire for a "free ride." Who could deny that he deserves it?

Mr. Maurice makes an excellent cheerleader, whose enthusiasm for someone else's ambitious efforts knows few bounds. He honestly, truly wants you to succeed; and if you should happen to become indebted to him in the process, as a result of his surreptitious efforts on your behalf, all the better. His pocketbook is always open to incoming transactions, and he welcomes all you care to provide in return.

Naturally, if you fail to reimburse him appropriately for those deeds that help pave the way to your career, your promotion, your biggest deal, some harsh punishments become inevitable. As many a recalcitrant underling on the way up has learned to his or her great displeasure, Mr. Maurice is well equipped with a whip for each hoof, each one sharpened to a needle-like point and ready to dispense some lessons of encouragement.

Editor's Note: One point must be clarified before leaving this subject: his whips and threats. Though he would be horrified to have this revealed, Mr. Maurice is most emphatically more bark (oops, oink) than bite. While he cultivates an aura of menace and danger, so as to intimidate his countless inferiors, underneath the surface he is actually a most gentle soul who would never harm a flea.

Not that he personally *has* any fleas, of course. As we see throughout these pages, Mr. Maurice is a pig of impeccable cleanliness and hygiene.

□

3

Mr. Maurice and Money

Does Maurice like money? Not at all. He *loves* money. Plenty of it. Money? You bet. He'll keep stuffing his (pardon the expression) piggy bank as long as you supply the contents. "Keep those bucks coming, and fast," he often announces.

Mr. Maurice's attitude toward money is simple and straightforward. He wants it. As much as he can get his hoofs on. Whenever a check comes into our home, delivered by the postman, you can be sure Mr. Maurice's hoof is out, awaiting his cut. Or better yet, the whole thing. Just sign it over to Mr. M., please.

To be blunt, he is one greedy little pig.

This is a distressing development, because he resides in a home whose occupants live simply, with few possessions, and seldom think or worry about money. His human companions cannot understand how Mr. Maurice could have become such a covetous little creature. Worse yet, he's *proud* of being a greedy pig.

Mr. Maurice's shopping list, in contrast to theirs, is invariably large, grandiose, and growing. No one knows exactly what potential delights it contains. We only know that if Mr. Maurice is denied too many of the goodies he's carefully listed, he becomes cranky and ornery. Sometimes, he's even inclined to try and bite your hand, if it contains no check or bank notes for him.

Now and then, he will even threaten to move to new quarters, to live among humans who share his avaricious motivations and will ensure that he continues to enjoy a vibrant, expansive lifestyle – the kind to which he has become inordinately accustomed in his present abode.

Oddly, most members of Mr. Maurice's extended piggie family are far less grasping and money-hungry. In fact, they seldom mention money at all. They appear entirely content to reside in comfortable surroundings among a congenial group of happy little pigs. With the exception of their lord and master, Mr. Maurice, that is, who seldom ceases to moan about his alleged near-poverty.

For Mr. Maurice, a happy family – while desirable and satisfying – is simply not good enough. Sadly, he is envious of all the greedy humans he observes on the TV. He envies the real people in the news, from financial barons and Wall Street wizards to questionably-talented celebrities who are paid bountifully for doing little (an ideal situation, in his view), right down to the characters in dramas who manipulate and maneuver so that they will come out ever wealthier in the end.

Mr. Maurice once saw the movie *Wall Street* on TV, and failed to understand why some humans were critical of Gordon Gecko, the avaricious character portrayed by actor Michael Douglas, for proclaiming that "greed is good." To Mr. Maurice, that's a simple, unassailable truth. How could anyone object to such a hard-and-fast fact?

More to his liking are the words of Fred C. Dobbs, as played by Humphrey Bogart in the classic 1948 film *The Treasure of the Sierra Madre*. After struggling for months to dig gold out of the Mexican mountains, his colleagues are ready to leave their mine with a windfall of $20,000. Not Fred (Humphrey). "Small potatoes," he snorts with disdain. Mr. Maurice could not agree more.

□

4

Mr. Maurice and TV

One critical fact quickly became evident when Maurice arrived at our home: He loves TV. *All* TV. Lots and lots of TV. He could watch TV day and night – and often does.

Yes, Maurice enjoys serious programming, classic films, concerts, documentaries. Yet in the dead of night, or whenever he thinks no one is looking, he may also be observed avidly viewing the most inane reality shows and the most moronic quiz programs. In short, his list of favorites appears to run the entire gamut, from *Gilligan's Island* reruns and *Survivor* episodes to in-depth news analyses and expertly-crafted modern dramas.

Because he has an intense opinion about everything, and is of course always correct in his appraisal of a situation, he especially enjoys the commentators on the news. "Aha!" he oinks, as soon as one of them makes what he perceives to be a grievous error of interpretation, omits what he knows to be a salient fact, or interjects a personal opinion without sufficient basis.

Naturally, because Maurice is a liberal intellectual pig, he becomes livid if Fox News happens to appear on the small screen. His normally delicate pink pelt begins to turn flaming red, his wide-spaced nostrils grown even farther apart, a front hoof pounds the air with derision. When he's particularly incensed by what he sees and hears, all four hooves have been known to rise into the air, turned into temporarily twitching arrows of disagreement.

Mr. Maurice takes this stuff seriously.

For that reason, he likes to sit back and relax with a lightweight comedy, or one of his raucous and snarky "guilty pleasures" in video. In fact, in addition to having full access to the family's store of DVDs and old VHS tapes, Maurice has a secret stash of his favorites – the ones that make him chortle and smirk and snort – tucked away somewhere at the rear of his reclining space.

"Mindless TV has its place," Maurice restates periodically. "It relaxes the brain, and lets it work even better." Not that his own brain could possibly work any better than it already does, of course.

Oddly, Mr. Maurice complains only occasionally about the fact that his home contains only one TV set, and it's an old one with a cathode-ray tube rather than a modern digital configuration. Perhaps it's because, underneath everything, he is a traditional pig, more concerned with what appears on the screen than how it's viewed. Yet, on occasion when passing a retail outlet, he's been known to gaze longingly at the biggest, baddest flat-screen TV in the store window.

☐

5

Mr. Maurice and Movies

Although Maurice is an authority on classic cinema, he also can be observed viewing far less impressive works. He says it's to maintain perspective. But the sly grins and chortles, barely seen and heard, appear to affirm his perverse appreciation for junk on film.

Although he abhors violence in everyday life, he's not above watching action movies – including some that are frightfully violent. That's because he absolutely *loves* movies. *All* movies. Almost as much as TV.

If he could, he would watch movies all day, every day, into the night.

As the supreme potentate, however, he has certain duties – not particularly taxing but necessary – to perform between rest periods. So, he reluctantly turns the DVD player's remote control over to his human consorts periodically.

One helpful benefit stems from his physical nature. Mr. Maurice has the admirable and convenient facility to see and hear movies whether he is actually viewing them or not. Or, whether the DVD player is turned on or not.

As a result, his store of cinematic lore and knowledge is unmatched by that of any mere mortal.

Ask him who played the hapless young husband in *The Bachelor Party* (1957), and he knows. He can also tell you who wrote it, who directed it, and the name of the actress portraying the insecure sophisticate at the party. Maurice's favorite film is the previously-mentioned *The Treasure of the Sierra Madre* (1948). He's fascinated by this timeless tale of hunting for gold, and by the descent of the aforementioned Fred C. Dobbs (Humphrey Bogart) into madness before he loses his head to a machete.

Maurice also loves Paul Newman as *The Hustler* (1962). Clearly, Maurice sees himself in that role as the ambitious up-and-comer taking on the top player. "Nearly all of life's lessons are in those two movies," Maurice often says. "It's as if I wrote them myself."

□

6

Mr. Maurice and the Opposite (Sex)

Because this is such a delicate matter, Maurice has difficulty even saying or writing that three-letter word. He speaks it in a barely-discerned whisper. Note the use of smaller characters for the word itself in the title above: a direct order from Mr. Maurice himself.

As anyone might imagine after gazing upon his handsome countenance, he is truly a lady's pig. Yet, Mr. Maurice is as discreet as they come.

No lady – pig or person – who has enjoyed his amorous attention need ever fear that their dalliance will become public. Mr. Maurice would rather be boiled in oil – or made to toil – than give out even a hint of detail about his romantic undertakings.

Because Mr. Maurice wears no pants, some observers have noted that he appears to lack a particular physical attribute that is generally considered essential to intimacy. He is quick to reassure us all that such is not the case.

"Appearances deceive," he is fond of asserting, with a sly wink. Suffice to say that when the situation calls for action, he is more than ready to comply. The squeals of delight that inevitably emanate from his paramour of the moment serve as an indisputable testament to his endowment and prowess. No one who has spent quality time with Mr. Maurice, he points out with uncharacteristic immodesty, has ever left his embrace dissatisfied.

☐

7

Mr. Maurice and Knowledge

Few would argue with the fact that Mr. Maurice's level of knowledge is complete and perfect. If anyone did deign to take exception to this indisputable claim, Maurice just might invite that denier to step into the alley for further discussion on the subject. Before accepting such a challenge, it would be wise to note that while he is most emphatically a nonviolent pig, Maurice also is thought to possess certain little-seen physical skills – including a high standing in the martial arts. Consider yourself warned.

Obviously, it's handy to have such a pig (or person) around. But it's frustrating, too. By definition, after all, Mr. Maurice always wins any argument, and then mocks you for even a minuscule, fleeting attempt to question his assertions.

The more you know, the more you grow. That's Mr. Maurice's motto for everyone. Obviously, since he cannot possibly know any more (though he could perhaps grow a bit), the rule does not apply to himself, personally.

Mr. Maurice, however, is seriously miffed by the proliferation of alleged knowledge on the Internet. Quantity, he insists, has nothing at all to do with quality. Neither does speed. Near-instantaneous access to information simply clutters the brain, Maurice asserts, mainly with useless bits of fluff and trivia. And worse yet, with erroneous information. During encounters with Mr. Maurice, don't ever make the mistake of beginning a sentence with: "I saw on the Internet that...." Or, "I got a tweet that said...." Maurice will lose not a moment in making sure you are aware of your error, and that you never forget that transgression.

Shocking as it sounds, even Mr. Maurice cannot always tell the difference between an accurate, true statement and a scrap of imposing-sounding nonsense on a website, a Twitter tweet, or a texted message. His brain is too mighty to be bothered with trying to assess such distinctions. If Maurice is unable to discern what's correct as opposed to what is not, what hope could there be for the rest of us?

☐

8

Mr. Maurice and Misbehavior

"String 'em up!"

That would be Mr. Maurice's answer and solution to a slew of misdeeds, large and small. Being a nonviolent pig, of course, he does not necessarily mean that this concise plea is to be taken literally. On the other hand, his face does betray tiny hints of enjoyment when he utters that trio of words. One could easily imagine Maurice wielding the rope himself, lassoing the miscreants and tossing the end of the lariat over a tree branch of appropriate height. Or, since he is an urban pig, over a street sign on a crowded downtown street in the culprit's own city.

Ah, but that's merely a momentary taste of fantasy revenge slipping out. Naturally, as a nonviolent porker, Maurice has no desire to bring an end to any person's – or pig's – mortal existence. Therefore, he posits alternatives, such as tying the offender to a tree so that he or she may be subjected to stern verbal abuse from Mr. Maurice himself, as well as from his cabal of underpigs.

Mr. Maurice is glad to inflict punishment on others, be it a wit-riddled tongue-lashing or more harsh physical exertions. Needless to say, he never deserves the slightest penalty himself, from pig or person.

Shocking as it may appear, however, Mr. Maurice has been known to misbehave. He refers to his antics as "controlled misbehavior," and therefore harmless. Still, the sight of this pink porcine creature dancing around, tossing his hooves high into the air, almost losing his beret as he struts and cavorts before any audience that happens to be present, is oddly disconcerting. To some observers' eyes, it's downright undignified, if not uncivilized. More on Mr. Maurice's lapses in dignity in the next chapter.

□

9

Mr. Maurice and Dignity

Nothing is more important to a pig (or to a sophisticated person) than dignity. Yet, alive or otherwise, pigs have been, and continue to be, subjected to any number of undignified situations.

Mr. Maurice intends to put a stop to this unseemly activity.

What, he asks, could be more vital and ultimately satisfying than maintaining one's dignity. He who does so in the face of troubles and assaults is a force to be reckoned with.

Needless to say, Maurice would be such a force regardless. Dignity is what allows a person – or a pig – to stand tall, able to weather the most outrageous affronts, yet know he or she is on the correct course.

A mere glance informs anyone that Mr. Maurice is one totally dignified pig, in every respect. Even on those rare occasions when he has been observed cavorting in seemingly undignified actions, largely to impress his many lady friends, he does so with an air of dignity beneath the surface. Yes, even when flat on his back on the floor, being tickled and titillated by a flock of female admirers, Mr. Maurice manages to maintain a dignified bearing. However, he does not suggest that any lesser creature try to emulate such behavior. "They would just look stupid and unseemly," he warns.

So many pastimes and pursuits are undignified these days, even if participants don't realize it – or, all too often, simply don't appear to care. Avoid undignified positions at all costs. That's Maurice's unqualified recommendation. Onlookers will remember any offenses to decency indefinitely, and Maurice surely does not wish his reputation sullied. Neither should you.

◻

10

Mr. Maurice and Guilt

Naturally, Mr. Maurice is guilty of nothing. How could he be, since everything he does is rational and orderly. Therefore, all that he knows about the sensation of guilt applies only to others. No argument there.

If anyone has nothing to be guilty about, that would be Mr. Maurice. In order to feel guilt, one has to have done something wrong. Something bad. Something harmful. Can anyone imagine Mr. Maurice engaging in such an activity, even inadvertently? Perish the thought!

Now, that doesn't mean Mr. Maurice is the least bit hesitant about inflicting guilt upon *you*. That is his forte. Whether deserved or not, once you enter his domain, his presence, you can be sure he'll come up with something you might have done along the way that warrants guilt – and most likely, requires that you make amends to his benefit. Clearly, you deserve such punishment regardless of the details, simply by virtue of your not being *him*.

Remember, there's a vast difference between having guilt feelings and *being* guilty. Feelings of guilt should be reserved for the truly guilty, Maurice asserts – of a crime, or bad behavior, or bad taste in dress or form.

Yet most guilt feelings, in Maurice's estimation, result from thoughts and actions that don't deserve such self-abuse; or at least, not that much. What is the point of feeling guilty about thoughts and behavior that are normal?

Maurice has noted that several of the major religions are especially adept at inducing their followers to feel guilty about one thing or another. Or, about most things. Certain cultures also have developed that facility. Maurice takes strong exception to such practices, having observed that the worst actual offenders against society typically don't appear to feel guilty at all.

As for lascivious or nasty thoughts, Maurice observes that we all have these, so there's certainly no need or reason for anyone to try and instill guilt feelings. "If they knew what passes through my own monumental mind," he says, "they'd be shocked beyond belief." Yet, Maurice feels no guilt or shame at all for what amount to normal thoughts.

□

11

Mr. Maurice and Politics

Until pigs are permitted to run for office, alive or otherwise, Mr. Maurice holds little hope for the future.

Because Maurice is so disgusted by the activities among human political leaders, he has elected to concentrate on narrow local issues. He is a staunch advocate of barnyard politics – provided, of course, that he is the undisputed head of the barnyard, and it's sufficiently large and notable.

No correct-thinking pig would ever have supported Mr. Bush as leader, he points out. His hopes have been markedly higher for Mr. Obama, but he soon became dismayed by the loud and vociferous obstructionists, and has not entirely been pleased by the President's actions, either.

Pigs would never behave that way, he says. Even when his own dictates are disagreed with, he listens to the opposition – and then, of course, does exactly what he had in mind, regardless.

Maurice believes that a third party is definitely needed, and that it should be the Pig Party. By that he doesn't mean it would be limited to pigs, but his fellow porcine creatures should participate in the lion's share – that is, the pig's share – of planning and decision-making. He's certain this is the only solution to the ills that plague the current political system: corruption, self-serving legislation, pandering to the lowest common denominator, favoritism, fearmongering, the sowing of racial intolerance, warmongering.

That's quite a list of horrific political behavior that Maurice has come up with, and it's so rampant in the 21st century. When he hears the name-calling that takes place, he's reminded of a schoolyard where the bullies have taken over, leaving the other children to cower in fear.

Naturally, Mr. Maurice has researched politics of the past, and is both dismayed and pleased to see that the vile attacks that plague the current political climate are nothing new. In fact, some of the attacks heard on TV pale in comparison to the vicious assaults made by politicians of the distant past.

12

Mr. Maurice and Inequality

As long as they realize that some pigs are, as Mr. George Orwell once observed, "more equal than others," every pig (and person) is equal to the next, in Maurice's eyes. (Readers unfamiliar with Mr. Orwell's tome, *Animal Farm*, may be reminded that the pig who happened to serve as leader of the group deemed himself to be the one who stood above the herd in terms of equality, based upon his overall excellence compared to the rest.)

Be that as it may, Mr. Maurice is utterly dismayed to realize that entire groups of humans are treated harshly, because they're different in some way. How can this be, he asks.

Maurice does not say everyone should be treated the same, because everybody isn't the same. But he's aghast at the vast gulf between the top and the bottom. Why, the rich and powerful have nearly everything, and still want more. Those at the bottom struggle to amass a few crumbs, and – often as not – they're derided and vilified by many of their "betters," essentially for being poor. Upper-level workers are sought-after, flattered, and offered even more remunerative positions. Bottom-level workers are ignored, passed over, humiliated. None of this would ever happen in the barnyard, Maurice maintains.

13

Mr. Maurice and Citizenship

Because of some nonsensical rule about having to be alive to be a citizen, Mr. Maurice does not vote himself. Even so, he is highly active politically and – no surprise to his many friends, as well as opponents – never short on political opinions. These he expresses with his customary candor and relish, inevitably disarming and vanquishing those irrational thinkers who dare to espouse alternate viewpoints.

Some may say this is precisely what the Republicans in America have done since the first moment of the Obama Administration. True, but for one vital difference: Mr. Maurice is (of course) absolutely right in his political statements.

How could he not be? He is Mr. Maurice.

Despite his lack of personal voting experience, Maurice takes the notion of citizenship seriously indeed. He only wishes that more of the official citizens would do likewise.

Not that merely voting is enough. Far from it. In Mr. Maurice's clearly-developed view, an uninformed vote is worse than no vote at all.

Civics classes are needed now more than ever, he says, yet they seem to have been slipping out of the curriculum at so many schools. Maurice blames the schools for the current lack of civic knowledge – not the teachers, to be sure, but the administrators, the "big boys" in charge of what is to be taught.

"Pay attention" to what's happening in the country and the world, Maurice warns. Express opinions, don't hide them or just whine about how awful things have gotten. Maintaining democracy takes effort and thoughtful participation, so we're not swayed by the falsehoods and distortions that candidates toss out on TV. Like everything else that's worth keeping, he adds, "use it or lose it."

☐

14

Mr. Maurice and Luxury

This is an easy one. Mr. Maurice simply *loves* luxury. He revels in it, savors it, practically demands it.

On the one hand, he's fond of claiming that he is really, underneath it all, just a *cerdito pobre* (poor little pig). But in reality, he would be more than pleased to enjoy every moment of his existence in supreme luxury, posh and perfect.

In his view, spending each day attended to by servants, his every whim addressed within moments of its discovery, is the only appropriate scenario for one of his stature. His image of daily life even goes a step further, to include a bevy of voluptuous beauties, clad in diaphanous gowns that conceal little of their shapely endowments, who serve him enthusiastically and eagerly simply because there is nowhere else they'd rather be.

Yes, plenty of poshness is the rule. A person or a pig can never have too much luxury, as far as Mr. Maurice is concerned.

On the other hand, he would like to see those folks who have little or nothing get an occasional taste of luxury, too. He believes luxury, even in limited quantities, is good for the soul. He's also certain that most of the impoverished and downtrodden folks among us would appreciate a few luxuries more than those who have it all the time.

What Maurice detests, however, is phony luxury. He can't stand to have service persons fawning and flattering guests, while secretly despising them. Though he cannot be certain that such employees have such a harsh opinion of the people with whom they deal, he's willing to bet that most of them do, and that they're inwardly laughing at those who are being flattered.

Of course, those attitudes would not apply to Maurice himself, who deserves and savors every bit of flattery that anyone could possibly come up with.

□

15

Mr. Maurice and Opinions

If you and I agree on everything, the saying goes, one of us is unnecessary. Maurice endorses that truism, though he has no doubt as to which participant, in an exchange of ideas between himself and another, would be the one "to go."

Obviously, Mr. Maurice's opinions are infallible. But what of those from lesser folk that are simply good. Or thoughtful. Or well-reasoned. How do they stand up to scrutiny by the master pig?

Those who are in the business of formulating and disseminating opinions on one subject or another must be wary, Maurice warns. They cannot forget that their own opinions, no matter how firmly based on fact and reality, are nonetheless only that: opinions. Not many issues exist that cannot be viewed in more than one way.

Even in elemental politics, those on the far left or right can never truly say their views are the one and only correct positions. That is true only if certain basic attitudes toward life itself exist. A progressive liberal cannot be anything else if he or she believes that we all have a duty toward the less fortunate, and to those who differ from us. An ardent conservative cannot be otherwise if he or she believes that one's own group takes precedence, and that business is the proper foundation of modern life.

Maurice notes that this is why political arguments – attempts to sway another person – are doomed to failure.

If a person's (or pig's) inner principles are well thought-out and firmly held, being swayed to the other side is an impossibility. The sole exception would be when indisputable new information is brought to light, which may impact one's basic principles and positions.

Otherwise, only those who *lack* inner principles can conceivably be brought to one side or the other, and their newly-acquired preferences will be based on a shaky foundation. To illustrate this point, Mr. Maurice points directly to political commercials on TV, designed to influence voters by distortion, falsehoods, and trickery. To Maurice's masterful mind, only those viewers who are incapable of independent thought, or too lazy to attempt it, can be swung from one side or one candidate to the other. Is this the kind of democracy we want, he asks, based upon ignorance? He hopes not, but the evidence of late is clearly in the other direction.

□

16

Mr. Maurice and Empathy

Maurice frequently expresses concern for the disadvantaged, the troubled, the needy. On rare occasions, he has even been known to dig deep in his own pocket (never actually seen by anyone) to extract a donation to a worthy cause or individual. Even though it does not beat like those of other creatures, Mr. Maurice has a true "heart" where it counts.

That said, we must never lose sight of the fact that his inherently greedy nature prevents Mr. Maurice from digging all that deep, all too often. Giving to another, after all – however worthy the recipient – means that much less for one who is worthy above all. Namely, himself.

Frankly, Maurice doesn't see much empathy rolling around these days, at least among the "better people." So many of the well-off, he observes, see the world as being all for themselves, with nary a thought for those who didn't make it up the success ladder. Instead of a hand up, those forlorn folks are more likely to get a quick shove back down.

How can this be, Maurice asks often. Despite his greatness, Maurice feels empathy for every last one of his lessers – which of course includes everyone: rich, poor, and at every stage in between.

☐

17

Mr. Maurice and Secrecy

Oh, yes. Mr. Maurice simply *loves* secrets. He's good at keeping them, too. At least, we all *think* he is.

Actually, Maurice fancies himself a spy of sorts – one who can be trusted to maintain the deepest and darkest of secrets, disclosure of which could put the entire world in jeopardy. Why bother with trifling secrets, he would ask, when so many biggies are out there, just waiting for himself to find out about them. And of course, keep tight-lipped about them afterward.

Not that he is above zeroing in on little personal secrets. Sad to say, the sophisticated Mr. Maurice is also on occasion one gossipy little pig. This is one of his few failings.

Tell him your most innermost hidden thoughts, and you can practically bet he won't blab them all around. Unless an element of personal gain enters the picture, that is. Yes, greed does occasionally overtake Mr. Maurice's more appealing traits.

He does occasionally feel guilty about revealing other people's (or pigs') secrets – and he will never leak even a hint of his own secrets, of course. Yet, when he believes his pocketbook may be running low, he cannot always restrain himself from making use of some little morsel of information to which he's been given ostensibly secret access. Secretly, he's sometimes said he would rather *not* know others' secrets, so as to avoid temptation.

Maurice actually appears to have many secrets of his own. At least, his sly grin when queried about such matters suggests a secret stash of secrets.

Viewing the subject another way, Maurice does not like to have his movements, his preferences, too widely known. He certainly does not wish to be tracked in any way, by computer or otherwise. Should you be discovered while trying to glean information about him, Mr. Maurice affirms that he will deal harshly with your offense. Remember, those needle-point whips of his are always at hand (or more accurately, at hoof), poised to deliver a searing and long-lasting message in response to your misdeed.

□

18

Mr. Maurice and Waste

Unfortunately, Mr. Maurice is not as "green" as his countless admirers might suspect. Most of them perceive him as an ardent environmentalist, concerned about the future of the planet and taking regular steps to make a difference for the coming generations.

Sadly, that is not necessarily the case. Mr. Maurice often is tempted to waste. Nearly always, he is able to resist. But now and then, he gives in to temptation. In fact, he revels in that temptation and is, we regret to report, sometimes notorious for his profligacy.

This is embarrassing to report. At times, Maurice almost seems to *enjoy* excess and waste, flaunting his evident lack of concern for the world around him.

How can this be? Some of us believe it's because he just can't abide being told what to do, even if he agrees that reducing the amount of trash we produce is a fine thing.

After all, he sometimes suggests – though his wary smile lets the onlooker know that he knows he's fooling himself – because Maurice is acknowledged to be the supreme intellect of the world, should he really have to abide by the daily, humdrum rules of civilized life?

Well, of course he should. He knows that, and catches himself, realizing yet again that not only is leading a non-wasteful existence the right thing to do, but he must set an example for the rest of us. He must serve as a role model for those of lesser intellect and therefore, reduced understanding of the requirements of civilized behavior. He promises that in future, he will do his best.

Maurice does recycle, though the extra effort makes him a tad grumpy. Especially since he's not entirely certain that the recycled items go anywhere special. Maybe they all wind up in the same dump, or the same landfill, as ordinary garbage. He's heard and read the stories about such practices.

Naturally, he is not about to approach a garbage truck himself, much less a dump, since they are so smelly and unclean. He squirms and winces at the very thought of being in close proximity to such a place. He admires those who haul away his trash, he certainly would not want to be in their shoes – or their hooves, as the case may be.

☐

19

Mr. Maurice and Communication

Because Maurice has such a wide network of friends and

admirers all over the world, you'd think he would be a devotee of instant communications. Surely, he must possess the very latest of cell phones – most likely, a model that's a step beyond what is currently available to the general public, with features that only he knows how to access and operate.

In that assumption, you would be mistaken. Maurice prefers to communicate the old-fashioned way: by yelling and bellowing at his underlings. Communication, to Maurice, is strictly a one-way street: orders emanating from himself, and no back talk permitted to annoy him, in the other direction.

But what about instant communication with those he doesn't know – the followers and fans. He has so many, true; but that doesn't mean he wishes to exchange views with them. Certainly, not at this very moment. Furthermore, why would he wish to consider their opinions when his own are so masterful and cogently articulated? That would be like mixing roses and fine wine with wallowing swine.

(Oops! Maurice demands that the last metaphor be cancelled immediately. Make that "mixing roses and fine wine with wallowing beasts.")

Asked about texting and tweeting, Maurice admits that he enjoys condensing his virtuoso thoughts and statements into abbreviated messages. He sees it as a mental challenge, sure to make his own brain even more magnificent. Yet here too, all of his messages are outgoing-only. We may live in a world where everyone is encouraged to comment on everything, instantly; but Mr. Maurice does not care to hear what you have to say, with the possible exception of words that are of a strictly admiring nature.

Maurice prefers hearing the news on TV to reading the newspaper (though he does both, most days). He admits to being almost infatuated with MSNBC's Rachel Maddow, but he tries to take in viewpoints from every perspective.

After watching and hearing so many commentators on TV, however, Maurice has determined that he, himself, wishes to be the prime pundit. Who better, since he knows it all – which is far more than he can say for most of the "talking heads" that he sees on his screen.

□

20

Mr. Maurice and Fine Dining

Some foolish critics allege that because Mr. Maurice lacks innards in the usual biological sense, and therefore possesses no digestive system, he cannot possibly eat at all, much less enjoy culinary pleasures on a lofty scale.

"Nonsense," he scoffs. Mr. Maurice enjoys nothing more than a carefully created, magnificently served meal – preferably one of substance and heft, for which someone else is carrying out (or has completed) the actual work of preparation. Maurice invariably prefers to enjoy the result of another's culinary art, not tire himself out trying to duplicate any such efforts.

Mr. Maurice Knows It All ... and tells you so

Mr. Maurice is particularly bewildered by the sort of restaurant where the customer participates in the cooking of a steak or other entree. "If I wanted to work in order to eat, I would have stayed home," he explains.

Candles are *de rigueur* when Mr. Maurice is ready to be seated at table for a culinary experience. He further insists on a pristinely clean, white tablecloth and white linen napkins. No paper napkins for Mr. Maurice, please. Tuxedoed waiters, when available, round out the evening. At the very least, they should be immaculately dressed. Maurice would be aghast if presented with a filet mignon or *coq au vin* by a serving person wearing torn jeans and gym shoes. In fact, he says he has occasionally had nightmares about just such a travesty.

Naturally, Mr. Maurice is a connoisseur of fine wines to accompany each dining experience, but he doesn't make an issue of it. In fact, when he hears a dinner companion begin to pontificate endlessly on the arcane merits of a particular vine or vintage, Maurice just might begin to oink his derision.

If you're going to dine finely, Maurice explains, go all the way. Sure, it's all silly, he adds; but it looks classy. And Maurice is one classy little pig, as we all know.

When he dines out, Maurice has two rules: no self-service, and no dishwashing afterward. Befitting a pig of his stature, he wishes to be waited on, hand and hoof, with proper servility.

Fine dining, needless to say, is specifically for when someone else is paying the bill. If Maurice must dig into his personal pocketbook, considerably less fineness will suffice.

21

Mr. Maurice and Humans

"Many of my best friends are humans," Maurice is fond of reporting. Still, he notes that he doesn't quite understand them – a shocking revelation from a pig who otherwise knows everything.

They're often so "piggish," he says with dismay, evidently unaware for the moment of the irony of using that particular word. Wasteful, unruly, surly. Hateful, ignorant – and yes, stupid. Not all of them, to be sure. But far too many, he insists, shaking his head with a dejected frown evident below his snout.

Naturally, Mr. Maurice dislikes uttering such a harsh assessment of fellow creatures, inferior though they may be to the likes of his magnificence. Clearly, he realizes that he stands far above the ordinary pig. But he also encounters few humans who share his lofty thoughts, his precision analytical mind, his refined demeanor.

Exceptions abound, to be sure: Gandhi, Einstein, Martin Luther King. Great artists, composers, performers. Economist Paul Krugman, whose discerning opinions and recommendations make it clear to Mr. Maurice that he should be in full charge of the country. Looking to the past, Maurice cites such figures as Eugene Debs and Cesar Chavez, for their work in favor of the workingman. Today, he favors Nicholas Kristof, writing cogently and insightfully from many of the globe's trouble spots. Independent Senator Bernie Sanders. Lots of exceptions to the sad rule of unthinking humans.

Early in 2011, Maurice was especially impressed by former Senator Olympia Snowe, who chose not to seek re-election when she realized the extent to which the far right had taken over her Republican party. Dick Durbin. Franklin Roosevelt. Pete Seeger. Bruce Springsteen. To the surprise of some, Maurice has kind words of praise for Lady Gaga, for her work to prevent bullying of schoolchildren. And many more from elsewhere in the world.

Yet, so many intolerant, hateful types come to the forefront that Mr. Maurice is distressed – and he does not like to be distressed! Rush Limbaugh, Glenn Beck. Even Rick Santorum, who appears to be a gentler soul yet espouses 19th-century views that give Maurice shivers. "What's wrong with them," Maurice continues to wonder. Keep the immigrants out, so many of them shout. Give rich humans all they want, even if it means taking from the poor.

What have the haters done to the gentle teachings of Jesus Christ, of Moses, of Mohammad. Maurice simply doesn't get it, which is something of a surprise. "Pigs would never act like that," he counsels. "Evidently, I just don't understand humans," he laments. "But how can that be, when I understand everything else?"

☐

22

Mr. Maurice and Daily Life

In view of the unprecedented magnificence of Mr. Maurice's mentality, you'd expect him to have a complex, detailed philosophy of life. Possibly with voluminous footnotes and annotations. Yet, his basic motto is simple: Take it easy. However, he also adds the late Mr. Studs Terkel's preferred suffix to that phrase: "But take it."

Maurice most definitely wishes to *take it*, whatever it is. Keep the bucks flowing in, he commands, greedily grasping for whatever checks, banknotes and even small change comes his way. Or, near his abode, as he is not above extending an eager hoof outward when he spies some dollars passing by the area.

A day without a substantial deposit into his pocketbook is simply not a day worth remembering, Mr. Maurice often advises.

Mr. Maurice rises late, lazily. Why? Because he is not obligated to do so early. Unless you have to get up early, he notes, may as well lie abed longer and get an extra beauty nap. Naturally, he adds immediately, a beauty nap is not really needed, since he is already as beautiful as possible.

Maurice generally stays up late to watch more TV, review his day, contact lady friends. He also is rumored to host virtually endless parties, though his household companions never seem aware of when they're happening. Sporadically, they can just barely detect a lot of light, yet rollicking sounds emanating from Maurice's residential area at the side of the living room, suggesting a fine time was being had by all. All the piggies, that is. Evidently, people are not invited to Mr. Maurice's special soirees.

□

23

Mr. Maurice and Family Life

Without question, Maurice rules his pen – his pig family – with compassion, but also with an iron hoof waiting behind. Regardless, he adores that sizable family, considering it vital to his well-being.

On the other hand, he places comparable value upon the families of others, which he believes to be the only reasoned approach. Gay families? Single parents? Rich families, poor ones. Living in Manhattan high-rises or starving in the Sudan. They're all the same to him. As long as they treat their young ones nicely, and bring them up well, he gives them a quadruple "hoofs up."

Mr. Maurice is dismayed by the claims that only a family consisting of a (male) husband and (female) wife will suffice. That's a pleasant situation as a rule, he admits. But hardly an essential one. After all, Maurice has no wife to help raise the little piggies in his sty. And look how well they're all turning out!

Certainly, one's personal family is important, but it's not everything. In Maurice's view, the global family, including all other people's children, is no less significant than one's own offspring. "Whatever you do to the least of us," he recalls, quoting biblical scripture, "you did it to me." Mr. Maurice is in full accord with that lofty yet elemental principle, and wishes far more of us would take its words seriously.

□

24

Mr. Maurice and Gambling

Mr. Maurice *loves* to gamble – provided that it's on a sure thing. "Why would I invest my hard-earned dollars on something that's not certain," he often asks – conveniently ignoring the fact that all the earning in his household is carried out by his human companions; he simply reaps the benefits of their labors.

He adores the horse races, in particular, because of the beauty of the animals as they race around the track, demonstrating once again to Mr. Maurice how pleasant it is to never have to work up a sweat. Or, better yet, to never push beyond a modest stroll, on those rare occasions when he's compelled to leave his comfortable seat for a short while.

Never is he tempted to bet, however, unless he's heard from one of his pig acquaintances who happens to reside near the stables, and can tell him exactly which steed is sure to be victorious on its next outing. Such assurances, while welcome, are seldom quite enough, of course. Therefore, he invariably seeks a second opinion; and even a third.

Mr. Maurice also studies the *Racing Form*, with a scholarly intensity befitting an esteemed historian delving into the elements of the Dead Sea Scrolls, or the origin of the pyramids of Palenque. Only when he is thoroughly satisfied that the race has virtually been run already, and "his" horse has emerged the victor, is he ready to twist open the strings of his purse and come up with a cash wager.

Mr. Maurice also loves Las Vegas. He enjoys the action, the color, the good-looking women – though female piggies are seldom seen on the casino floor, for some reason. Rarely does he indulge himself in a wager, though – certainly not one of any size. More than any analyst alive (or not alive, as the case may be), Mr. Maurice knows the odds. Does he ever! They are against him, he says with a blend of assurance and annoyance. Therefore, he will merely observe, and store up additional knowledge for future endeavors of a gambling nature.

He is especially taken with Texas Hold 'Em, which he views as the most serious game in the casinos, and therefore the only one deserving of his attention. He's almost ready to sit down with the top players, and especially admires Mr. Chris "Jesus" Ferguson – the bearded gentleman with shoulder-length hair who dresses all in black, with sunglasses and black cowboy hat. Like Mr. Maurice in his everyday attire, that particular poker-playing professional makes a lasting impression. Mr. Maurice admires that in a person – or a pig.

25

Mr. Maurice and Consumption

Does Maurice like to consume? Oh, yes. Given the opportunity – and a filled pocketbook – he can buy, and buy, and buy. The more, the better – as long as someone else is providing, that is.

Doesn't matter what it is, Maurice would like to have it. If not to consume it immediately, then to hoard it away for later. He is, as we know only too well, one greedy little pig.

For *you*, on the other hand, consumption should – indeed must – be far more modest. As an ordinary mortal, you are entitled to subsistence, he feels – to make sure you keep on working hard, so that he might benefit from the fruits of your labors. But anything more than the minimum should be at his own personal discretion.

Maurice happily recalls the film musical *Oliver*, in which Dickens' title character – residing in an orphanage – asks for "more" in the dining room. Every time he sees that request being denied, Maurice chortles just a bit. This callous reaction is shocking to witness, since Mr. Maurice is ordinarily a kindly and generous pig. But when it comes to getting more, versus getting less, Maurice will always be in the line that gets the biggest share. He does not expect to see you there.

26

Mr. Maurice and Status

Status is a difficult issue for Mr. Maurice to contemplate. After all, when you're at the very pinnacle yourself, with absolute Number One status in every respect, who cares where everyone else stands?

Actually, since he prizes precision highly, he *does* care about comparative status. In fact, Maurice pictures everyone lined up neatly, in perfect ascending order, with himself at the very tip-top.

The hierarchy of pigs is absolute. Of people, more ambiguous. Maurice likes these things spelled out clearly. In his view, *all* pigs deserve high status, relatively speaking. That's a given, because they are so much more trustworthy than humans.

In times of financial crisis, few expect to move upward – except for those new Status Seekers, successors to the strivers of the 1950s, who continued heading toward the top. At the same time, plenty of folks anticipate a downward slide. Maurice is bothered by this. Today, the uppermost group *knows* they're at the top of the heap. But if status is measured solely by dollars, what if someone accumulates more than Mr. Maurice? Is his Number One spot tarnished. Will he, too, start to skid downward?

Though he values high-end cars and luxury goods of all sorts, and would love to accumulate more and more of them, Mr. Maurice does not care for the idea of using commodities as indicators of status. "Too much ambiguity," he insists. Under certain circumstances, someone with ever-growing mounds of possessions might develop the appalling notion that he or she ranks close to Maurice in status! To nip this idea right in the bud, Mr. Maurice generally favors a classless society – again, with himself at the apex. How, he asks, could it ever be otherwise?

□

27

Mr. Maurice and Groups

With only a few exceptions, Maurice is not a joiner. Because he dislikes crowds, he tends to avoid groups of any sort – though he is intrigued by the anonymity that larger groups, in particular, typically offer. He is, as is widely-known, a highly private pig. He also worries about possible development of "groupthink," whereby all members start to think alike. After all, he warns, "what if they all began to take positions in opposition to my own?" His shoulders begin to shudder, and his hooves to tremble, at the very idea of such a phenomenon ever occurring.

For obvious reasons, Maurice will never be a part of any "work" group, which would suggest that he might actually have to undertake tasks like an ordinary toiling creature. Groups devoted to causes that he values highly would be more tempting, but he normally takes the cautious route. Besides, small groups, he has observed, inevitably *turn into* crowds when the participants and passersby learn that Maurice is in the area.

Naturally, he must always be the leader – which can be exhausting. Shared *duties* he endorses, though he expects to have none for himself. Shared responsibility is fine too, though there is always a danger of developing unfortunate ideas for which no one is deemed responsible. To avoid such complications, Maurice would rather have all of it, unless that responsibility becomes too taxing. Then, he will be happy to delegate.

But shared rewards? "Yikes," he responds. "No, no." Maurice must have the lion's share (i.e., the top pig's share) of all profits – or preferably, all revenues. Others may share in the losses and costs, but the financial rewards? Not a chance!

□

28

Mr. Maurice and Transportation

"Where are they all going, anyway?" That's what Mr. Maurice would like to know, when he observes the hordes of automobiles at a near-standstill on the nation's highways.

Maurice looked it up, to make sure he had all the facts right. Our Interstate Highway system began back in 1956, under the administration of the grandfatherly President Eisenhower, largely to provide a way to evacuate cities in a time of emergency. In those days, Maurice notes, emergency meant an attack by Communists, most likely from the Soviet Union. Only later, as the system expanded, did it become best known simply as a high-speed network of highways to allow people to get to their far-off destinations as promptly as possible.

What would those engineers and highway developers think now, Mr. Maurice asks. Standing at an overpass along any major urban Interstate at rush hour time – or in many cities, just about anytime – all that can be seen in at least one direction is a stagnant sea of automobiles. Plus a barrage of trucks, large and small. Many of those passenger cars are big ones, too – SUVs, full-size sedans, vans – typically holding only a passenger or two, with all the remaining seats dead empty.

When he does need to travel, Mr. Maurice prefers to take the train. He laments the fact that not many trains are left in North America, unlike Europe; but he is pleased to know that they remain an option for him. By taking the train, he can avoid the humiliating security checks at the airport, as well as the inevitable delays and the snug seats in Coach class.

On those occasions when driving is the prudent choice, Maurice loves to ride in the back seat – especially if it's a luxury model or a convertible – safely belted, of course. Despite his modest height, Maurice is able to see clearly out the windshield, and enjoys all the sights: trees, lakes, rivers, historical buildings, pretty girls. At home or away, Maurice invariably has an eye for the ladies, as is well-known to all.

□

29

Mr. Maurice and Games

Simply put, Mr. Maurice does not play games. Asked why, he's likely to trot out the title of one of Mr. Norman Mailer's novels: *Tough Guys Don't Dance*. Maurice would rewrite that title to say, serious guys – pig or person – don't play games.

Since Mr. Maurice is arguably the most serious-minded creature on earth, if not in the conceivable universe, how can he be expected to engage in frivolous pastimes. As an urbane and sophisticated pig, he steers clear of every sort of game and contest.

Naturally, if he *chose* to do so, for whatever reason, he could – and would – be victorious in any sort of contest. He does not so choose. In fact, he is especially aghast at the grotesque prevalence of addictive electronic and online games – and those who proclaim that such activities contribute to learning for the modern world and especially for the future. If true, Mr. Maurice wants no part of that future.

Still, several games have almost proved to be the exception. Mr. Maurice has played chess, which is of course an intellectual and serious game, thus one that should entice him. But because he is able to foresee all the possible plays, as quickly and accurately as either a computer or an expert human, chess failed to keep his attention for long. He got tired of announcing "checkmate" at some point in every game.

Poker, on the other hand – as we see in the chapter on Gambling – almost became a passion for Maurice some time back. Purely by chance, he caught an episode of the World Series of Poker on TV one day, and in minutes he was hooked. He began to play at every opportunity: among friendly pigs and persons, in organized tournaments, in dark apartments surrounded by dangerous-looking gentlemen. The fact that he won nearly every hand provided some hair-raising experiences for Mr. Maurice when the occasional opponent – backed by a thuggish compatriot or two – chose to challenge Maurice's veracity.

"Why, he practically accused me of cheating," Maurice wailed later on, after extricating himself from the risky milieu – as he always managed to do – by making intensive use of his personal charm and magnetism. Some of us suspect that he may have handed out a modest gratuity or two to one of the aggressive observers, to "look the other way," but nothing of that nature was ever proven. Thus, Mr. Maurice remains a short-lived, but notable, legend in professional poker circles, even though he hasn't played in a good long while. Now and then, however, we hear the riffle of a deck of cards emanating from his abode, and realize he may be pining for another chance at the table.

Still, to Maurice, all games are a waste of valuable time – unless they happen to yield winnings in dollars that can be put to quick use on his many shopping trips. And what does it ever matter who wins, except to set bragging rights. In Maurice's view, those may be earned in more worthy ways.

☐

30

Mr. Maurice and Science

Surprisingly, Maurice does not trust science. Not totally.

After all, a practical or theoretical scientist is likely to insist that not only does Maurice not know everything, but that he cannot possibly know anything. He is, after all, a stuffed pig. A veritable toy.

Naturally, Mr. Maurice cannot let such assertions stand. This one is so ... unpiglike. Only a human, he insists, could utter such a slanderous allegation.

Maurice actually pictures himself in a freshly-laundered white lab coat, making great discoveries to benefit both humankind and pigkind. Unfortunately, some of the tasks assigned to scientists – and to medical personnel – make Mr. Maurice a tad squeamish. Harsh chemicals, questionable bodily fluids, potentially dangerous powders lurking nearby. Those are not the substances with which he cares to surround himself.

Furthermore, staring into a microscope for hours on end isn't Maurice's idea of a good time. Not when there are so many cafes to hang out in, so many nightclubs to enjoy, so many park benches to occupy for the purpose of pondering ever-greater prospects for the future. So, he will let others do the experiments – the "dirty work," as it were – and wait until the results are in. At that point, of course, he is obligated to check to see if he just might be able to make a few, or possibly quite a few, dollars from those lesser scientists' efforts. Mr. Maurice is always looking for monetary returns, as we all know only too well.

One aspect of science, which has been in the forefront recently, makes the teeny pink hairs on Maurice's pelt stand at attention – often causing a tickling sensation that causes him to twitch. When Maurice hears the deniers of "climate change," the ones who insist that nothing has been shown to implicate people and their technology in the raising of global temperatures, he practically loses control of his faculties. He snorts, he waves his hoofs in the air, he practically leaps off the ground in anguish and, yes, anger.

"How can they be so ignorant?" he asks, not even bothering to maintain his customary gentle tone. Unless they mend their ways and start paying attention, those head-in-the-sand folks will be hearing more from Mr. Maurice, and they won't like what they hear. They may even begin to experience the crack of one of his needle-pointed whips, which are needed periodically to bring the more unruly purveyors of idiocy into line. Mr. Maurice would much rather sway them by reason and logic, but when those fail, he is ready with alternatives.

☐

31

Mr. Maurice and History

"History is more or less bunk," said industrialist Henry Ford (the first) to the *Chicago Tribune* newspaper in 1916. Ford believed that the only history of any value "is the history we made today."

No, no, not at all, Maurice insists. History is what made us all – people and pigs alike – what we are today. He is of course distressed by the lack of prominent pigs in the history books, but says, simply: "What can you expect when humans are in charge?"

Maurice is actually most interested in *pre*-history. He thinks the real rules of behavior were largely established well before the Greeks and Romans came along – all the way back to folks living in caves and hunting for their food.

Conflict, war as a "solution," conjugal relationships, even the elements of trade. All of these activities have histories that reach back toward the beginning of the human experience, Maurice insists. Not to mention such peculiarly modern behavior as painting one's face, piercing one's body, and adorning that body with jewels. Maurice especially likes to detect and criticize traces of primitive behavior in what are ostensibly modern pursuits and pleasures.

Though he certainly does not go as far as Mr. Ford in dismissing history, Maurice cautions against relying on it excessively. Despite his mighty intellect, he frequently does say "What's done is done."

As for Mr. George Santayana's assertion that those who do not learn from history "are condemned to repeat it," Mr. Maurice insists he is simply too brainy to let such a thing happen. But lesser creatures do need to be warned, he admits.

□

32

Mr. Maurice and Religion

Pigs know just where they stand with the earth, the heavens, and all else. No one is needed (apart from Mr. Maurice himself, that is) to tell them what to believe, or how to go about it.

While religion remains a mystery to him, Maurice would never stand in the way of anyone believing, preaching, and practicing a particular faith. That is, he would never object to your doing so, as long as you let everyone else follow their own paths – or no path at all. For those zealots who insist that their own religion is the one and only true faith, Mr. Maurice issues nothing but scorn.

"What's wrong with those people?" he's been heard to ask. "What could possess them to believe, to demand, that their religion is the right one and everyone else is wrong?"

What Maurice truly cannot fathom is how the admirable teachings of Jesus Christ, Mohammad, Buddha, Moses and other great religious leaders from long ago have been so distorted by so many of today's practitioners of various faiths. Instead of telling their followers how marvelous it is to be good and kind and compassionate, they deliver sermons and pronouncements that are more hateful than helping.

When Maurice first heard of clergymen who harmed young children, and pastors who engaged in indecent behavior at the very same time they condemned even slight transgressions committed by other people, he could hardly believe his ear. Had he been in charge, all of them would have been punished severely after the first offense was reported.

Almost as worrisome are those practitioners who use the faith of their followers to enrich themselves, whether in money, power, or both. Mr. Maurice is a tolerant pig, but such immoral behavior simply cannot be tolerated. Therefore, he will be ready with acutely-sharpened whips in each hoof, should he happen to encounter any of these charlatans.

□

33

Mr. Maurice and Vanity

"Vain? *Moi?*" Mr. Maurice is aghast at the very thought.

Facts are facts, after all. He is one splendid pig: *un cochon magnifique*, one might say if one were French. How could one be vain, when one is simply stating the truth.

Personal appearance counts, to be sure. He does like to preen, to look well-tailored and confident, ready to be admired. Maurice has been seen gazing into a mirror for what seemed like hours, touching up those last little details of his pelt, his snout, his ear, his ever-present beret – which must at all times be presented at a sufficiently jaunty angle.

Watching Mr. Maurice primp and then bask in his own personal beauty is often reminiscent of Tony Manero, John Travolta's character in the 1977 movie *Saturday Night Fever*. After working all week at a humdrum job, Tony would stand at the mirror to carefully touch up his hair, making sure every single strand stood precisely in place, in preparation for starring at another evening at the disco.

Disco may be dead, but Mr. Maurice can understand that level of intrigue with one's splendid appearance – especially when it's party time, and ladies will be present. Maurice would not wish to waste a single opportunity to be admired and adored by the females of each species.

□

34

Mr. Maurice and Social Media

What's social about it? That's Mr. Maurice's response to every mention of Facebook, Twitter, LinkedIn, YouTube, MySpace, or any of the social-media sites that have popped up in the past few years, several of them destined to make zillions of dollars for their creators.

Maurice has no Facebook page. No LinkedIn account. No YouTube videos of himself cavorting in odd places. He certainly doesn't "tweet" on Twitter; and if he did, he'd never admit to engaging in anything with such a childish name.

Technologically speaking, Maurice is an old-fashioned pig, and wishes to remain so. Not a technophobe, understand. Far from it. He understands how all the latest technology works, and could give the developers a few pointers himself. He is simply dismayed by the extent to which young folks, in particular, fall for the latest high-tech gadgets and "apps" and programs – many of which, in Maurice's well-informed view, are little more than fluff. Silly doodads that pass the time, but little else.

When he hears about Facebook "friends" and "fans," not to mention Twitter "followers," Mr. Maurice snorts and oinks loudly in disgust. Maurice, needless to say, has plenty of *real* friends, and even more *authentic* followers and fans. That should be obvious, for a pig of his caliber. Therefore, Maurice has no need, and certainly no desire, for "pretend" versions, which amount to no more than feeble simulations of actual cohorts.

Maurice is especially dismayed and incensed by the rapid rise of all this childishness via computer, which is treated as something oh-so serious by the media and much of the public. Watch out, all you 24/7 connected folks. He just might decide to begin to uninvent the whole social media experience. If anyone can do it, that would be Mr. Maurice.

☐

35
Mr. Maurice and Technology

Whether it's computers, iPhones, or any other high-tech devices, Mr. Maurice stands ready to give a thumbs-down with each hoof. (He does not explain how that is possible since his hooves have no thumbs, but that's a question for another day.)

One major complaint takes precedence. "These things are too complicated," Maurice laments. Strong words from someone with his immeasurable brain power. Yet, if even Mr. Maurice cannot turn on a device and get it to operate effectively, that device needs to be ignored and, preferably, discarded. Taken down from the shelves and consigned to the scrap heap. Period.

Furthermore, Mr. Maurice adheres tenaciously to the dictum: Just because something *can* be done, doesn't mean it *should* be done. And it certainly does not mean that thing *must* be done. Maurice, in fact, would extend that ruling by another step, observing that just because something can be made faster or smaller, doesn't mean it should.

Humans, he fears, are far too enamored with technology. Rather than concentrate on the essential elements of a task, and simply get down to business, they fret and fume about just *how* that task should be accomplished. Which little gadget is needed? Is the current model fast enough, or should we wait until the next generation? Do we have an "app" to do that?

(Mr. Maurice becomes livid when he hears the word "app," his normally pink countenance turning red with rage.)

Make no mistake, Maurice adores certain gadgets – provided they do something truly useful, or in an undeniably better way than what's gone before, and they really are "user-friendly." Developers need to ask themselves if what they're doing is worth doing at all, much less in any "improved" way – which typically means smaller and smaller, faster and faster. Few products make the cut, in Mr. Maurice's admittedly jaundiced view.

Making stuff so small that it's nearly impossible to use is not a step ahead, it's a leap backward. Neither is packing in so many added capabilities that the basic function is practically lost beneath a maze of "special features." Maurice's hooves can't begin to cope with teeny buttons, and even *his* brain grows dizzily delirious when forced to flit from one menu to the next, to undertake what should have been a simple task.

Mr. Maurice prefers to sniff roses along the paths he follows. Getting to the end quicker, and quicker yet, does not impress him at all.

Don't even get him started on the technology that evolved into automated phone calls, or "robocalls," all intended to get as many people as possible to part with their dollars, with the least expenditure of effort or money. He's not about to part with any funds from his pocketbook due to the cooing, cajoling words of an unsolicited, mechanized salesperson. He fervently hopes that you won't, either, so they'll all go away.

□

36

Mr. Maurice and Fun

Maurice likes to have fun. Preferably, all the time. One of his favorite pop songs, in fact, is Ms. Cyndi Lauper's *Girls Just Want To Have Fun*. Boys, too, Maurice adds. And pigs, especially.

But never to the exclusion of producing useful and remunerative work, Maurice cautions. Fun should, and must, be secondary to toil. Or, if you're unusually fortunate, work and fun might be mixed together in your daily life.

Still, he inquires often, what constitutes fun? Can you have fun alone? Should you? Many do, but not all of us. So, should fun be a group effort? More important, exactly how enjoyable must something be to qualify as fun?

Can work actually *be* fun? Should it be, when possible? Mr. Maurice is of two minds on that one. On the whole, Maurice prefers to keep the two separate. In his view, work entails expenditure of effort, whether physical or mental, making it less than fun as a rule. Yet, he will accept the notion of satisfaction – indeed, fun – from one's work, provided that the task is accomplished in suitable time. And of course, that any checks due him for your efforts arrive promptly at his pocketbook.

◻

37

Mr. Maurice and Relaxation

Now, this is one topic on which Mr. Maurice is indisputably the Number One, prime expert.

Rest and relaxation. R and R, as they say. Nobody does it better.

Maurice absolutely loves to relax. Does he ever! He would be content to be in a relaxed state virtually all the time, were it not for the need to stay abreast of changes in both the pig and person worlds. Though seldom known to lie down, he has mastered the art of relaxing while in an upright position. He can do so with eyes either open or closed, too, and whether he's cognizant of your presence or not.

Relaxation, then, is just the ticket for Mr. Maurice – but not so much for the rest of us, at least until we've completed our assigned tasks and made sufficient progress on a few more projects. Then, and only then, will we be entitled to relax without the threat of a stinging tongue-lashing and some harsh oinks from Mr. M.

□

38

Mr. Maurice and His Inferiors

For obvious reasons, this will be an especially short chapter in our collection of grand (and grandiose) thoughts from Mr. Maurice. "Where are they?" he inquires when the subject is brought up. Could there possibly *be* any? Inferior to Mr. Maurice? Why, he practically swoons at the mere suggestion of such a concept.

Reminding him that something like seven billion people inhabit the earth at present – in addition to who knows how many pigs – we cautiously broached the forbidden topic. We asked if it's logical that he alone should be the absolute superior creature in the world. Or, as he prefers to put it, in the universe. Can he really rank Number One in every single endeavor and measure of excellence?

Mr. Maurice scoffs and sneers at this audacious and offensive proposition: that he could be merely Number Two in some minor realm. "Nonsense," he snorts with ill-concealed fury – so unlike his ordinarily gentle, indeed genteel, nature. "There is only one Mr. Maurice." We could not argue with the truth of that eloquent statement. Case closed.

□

39

Mr. Maurice and Immigration

Maurice's dictum on the right to live and work where you please is simple: As long as you behave yourself, you should be able to go wherever you like, work anywhere that pleases you and has a job available, marry anyone you choose regardless of their citizenship, and on and on.

To be blunt, Mr. Maurice is flabbergasted that the situation is otherwise, particularly in this era of globalization and instant worldwide communication. "Are these people nutty?" he asks. What gives them the right to erect artificial barriers to keep out "foreigners."

Maurice also is astonished at the progression of anti-immigrant thought, particularly in America. Today, it's undocumented Mexicans who come to work and earn money, to help keep their families afloat. In exchange for risking their lives crossing the border, they're branded "illegal" and, when captured, deported like unwanted animals. Looking back at history, which Maurice often does, reveals comparable animosity directed against Jews and other "displaced persons" (often derided as "DPs") who arrived after World War II. Decades earlier, immigrants from Ireland were the ones who drew the most vociferous protest. "Who will be next?" Maurice asks, after recounting the involuntary "immigration" of slaves from Africa.

Where a person or pig is born and grows up is, let's face it, a matter of pure chance: an accident of birth. Mr. Maurice, for example, was born – or more accurately, knitted – in England. In London, to be precise. Yet clearly, as anyone can plainly discern, he is of French descent, based on appearance as well as manners and sophistication. In fact, he claims ancestry from nearly every part of the world. And he himself has resided in the United States since he was a veritable piglet.

Now, what if one of those piggies from the past had not been permitted to migrate, seeking more suitable pens in other locales when necessary (or desired). Why, Mr. Maurice might not have come into being at all! *Quelle horror!* he would cry out at such a barbaric notion. Perish the thought, and wash your mouth out with soap for uttering such heresy, he insists.

□

40

Mr. Maurice and Illness

Even Mr. Maurice has a "down" day now and then. Despite having no innards in the customary sense, and no evident infirmities of any sort, his overall health can dip a bit, not unlike lesser creatures.

To the troubled, the infirm, the afflicted, and the plain old sick, Mr. Maurice is universally known as Dr. Maurice. Whether he has ever actually completed a medical curriculum at a university is doubtful, but his treatment methods are widely known to work wonders. Furthermore, his bedside manner ranks with that of the most accomplished and trusted old-fashioned MDs.

In fact, plenty of those MDs come to Dr. Maurice for consultation, whether about their patients – the ones most difficult to diagnose – or their own personal maladies. They know Dr. Maurice always has a helpful answer waiting on his tongue: a course of action virtually guaranteed to yield results of a positive nature, if not rapid and complete recovery.

As Dr. Maurice is fond of saying, medicine is more art than science, and conventional medical training has unfortunate limits. In this, he resembles Dr. House on the TV show of that name: a fictional diagnostician flaunting unconventional behavior and less-than-courteous attitudes toward patients and colleagues. But in the end, Dr. House – and Dr. Maurice – are the ones that others turn to when the symptoms make little sense.

☐

41

Mr. Maurice and War

Maurice is unequivocal on this subject. He hates war.

Period. Case closed. Doesn't understand it at all.

Oh, he can accept the fact that thousands of years ago, people – like other creatures – fought each other for sustenance. But then, civilization developed. With it should have come the abandonment of warfare. Instead, warfare kept escalating.

Mr. Maurice is troubled by the current use of drones to kill alleged enemies, but reminds us that these weapons used to "kill from afar" are all extensions of primitive warfare. As soon as the first primitive man came along who could throw a rock really far and accurately, the notion of hand-to-hand, personal combat was doomed. Not that personal combat was a great thing. Still, it had a certain anguished symmetry that is absent from much of modern combat.

All these countries, all these politicians, seem to go to war at a moment's notice, Maurice observes. And why? So they can acquire more territory, more power, more of something. Mainly, however, they're just telling their enemies, by show of force, that "mine is bigger."

On a lighter note, Mr. Maurice came across an old comedy recording at an archive not long ago. He loves to recount the routine, which depicts the time "when football came to the University of Chicago," an institution widely-known for academic excellence but not so much for athletic endeavors. Says one of the comic figures, when confronted by a fierce-looking opponent who appears to be ready to induce bodily harm: "Can't we discuss this?"

Mr. Maurice also has been troubled by the killing of Osama bin Laden in 2011. Not so much the act itself, but the public reaction. While he strongly favors President

Obama and supports him most of the time, he says he felt queasy to hear the President applauded for giving the order to kill. Mr. Maurice is emphatic when he says killing is *never* something to be proud of, no matter how evil or vicious the victim had been. It may be justified, it might be deserved. But killing should never be a cause for pride.

Real power doesn't come from the barrel of a gun, in Maurice's view. No, it comes from the power of a brain. Or more likely, many brains.

Not that even the greatest aggregation of human minds could match what bulges within Mr. Maurice's beret-topped head, of course. Certainly, even the most brilliant political figure lags far behind Maurice in knowledge and wisdom. That's a given. Obviously, a large number of highly active brains would be needed to come up with a response that could come anywhere close to what Mr. Maurice could achieve and toss off all by himself.

Regardless, he believes that they should be trying. And trying harder. Human leaders need to make use of every last drop of brainpower they can muster – from themselves and from those advisors who surround them. They could also learn from the past and not keep on forgetting or ignoring it. Maurice is fond of Mr. George Santayana's dictum on that score, affirming that "those who do not learn from the past are doomed to repeat it." What he cannot understand at all is, why?

☐

42

Mr. Maurice and Sports

No, thanks. Maurice and sports do not mix.

If for no other reason, Mr. Maurice avoids sports and strenuous exercise because of the possibility that such an activity might make him sweat. Or perspire. Naturally, he prefers the latter word, which has a more fluid, genteel tone.

Better yet, he wishes to avoid the prospect of experiencing such a phenomenon, even though he is not entirely sure that his physical makeup – having been knitted rather than born – would be conducive to perspiring.

Furthermore, participation in sports often means being too close for comfort to other pigs or persons. Let's face it, can we possibly picture the urbane, sophisticated Mr. Maurice strutting in a locker room, vying for space with burly, perspiring athletes? Hardly. He does like to strut, true; but only in civilized circumstances.

Though not a participant, and far from a fan, Maurice will watch a sport occasionally on TV, provided that it appears to have some mental element and not be strictly a test of physical skills. As a demonstration of physical prowess and individual achievement, Maurice concedes that athletic endeavors have a valid purpose.

Of course, he veers far off the conventional mark in his attitude toward competitive team sports. To wit, he could not care less who wins – and certainly not which city or school's team happens to emerge victorious. No,

Maurice appreciates the artistic demonstrations of skill, but not the emphasis on winning at all costs, to benefit one's locale more than oneself.

Of course, when he sees a prime athlete on TV, Maurice invariably remarks that he could do the same thing, just as capably. He just doesn't want to. Not at this time. No one, needless to say, would dare to question the veracity of his proclamation.

Maurice is not fond of professional athletes, who reap fabulous salaries for playing a game. He especially deplores many of the professionals seen on TV, who behave – in his humble opinion – like rich, whiny brats. Mr. Maurice does not take kindly to brats, especially when they're wealthy. He also frets about the adulation shown by youngsters toward favorite athletes. Admire their skills, yes. But idolize and revere them? Maurice admires intensity among young people, but would rather see it directed toward more meaningful pursuits.

Getting down to specifics, at various times, Maurice has been intrigued by curling (though he's not quite sure how this event, with its broom-wielding players, qualifies as an actual sport). He's been stimulated by the ceaseless action of rugby. Then too, being a pig with an eye for the ladies, he's been known to gaze for long periods at episodes of women's volleyball, especially when played by ladies in skimpy swimsuits.

Naturally, he is known to his compatriots as a "sport," and even a "good sport." But that hardly means he is willing to strain himself in the participation of some physically-taxing contest. Nor does it mean he cares to watch and cheer along with "the boys" on a weekend afternoon.

43

Mr. Maurice and Education

He's for it. As long as the youngsters don't get any foolish ideas, such as reaching the same pinnacle plateau that Maurice occupies as they amass knowledge, he believes they should continue learning indefinitely.

But not merely in school, he adds. True knowledge – and especially, wisdom and reasoning – seldom emerge from a conventional classroom or textbook, whether in grade school, high school, or the university. Maurice has seen too many allegedly educated persons, even with postgraduate degrees, who cannot even hope to be called knowledgeable and wise beyond their narrow specialties.

Teachers should be among the highest paid workers in the land, Maurice believes. How can it be otherwise? Parents entrust their offspring to these purveyors of learning. Shouldn't they be the very best, and their individual educators remunerated accordingly?

When it comes to higher education for young people – or young pigs – Mr. Maurice is mystified. Why, he asks, isn't everyone entitled to the best possible education that can be provided. When he hears what parents have to pay to send a single child through college, Mr. Maurice practically falls off his chair.

Although he himself is a party pig, Maurice has misgivings about the "fun" atmosphere at many universities, where keggers and sundry misbehavior appear to take precedence over diligent study. Still, he realizes that young folks need to "let off steam," as it were; so he offers them a bit more leeway than would ordinarily be the case.

What really gets Mr. Maurice's dander up – and he does not like to observe rising dander – is the emphasis on education as preparation for a better job. Now, he would certainly like to see more people get higher-level positions and earn more money. After all, he might find a way to get a cut of their increased earnings.

Regardless, the purpose of education is learning to think and analyze and reason, Maurice insists with unaccustomed passion in his booming voice. If that's your goal, go to a trade school. Maurice endorses those wholeheartedly. Universities are supposed to function on a loftier plane, in Mr. Maurice's estimation, and classes are supposed to be difficult and worth the effort. When he hears about the fluffy, innocuous subjects that some students wind up "studying," the teeny hairs on Maurice's pelt immediately stand on end.

Mr. Maurice heartily endorses sabbaticals, and not just for college professors. Everyone should get "time off" periodically to study and learn a new subject, in a new place, under new conditions, he insists. Not so they can loaf around in exotic locales, he hastens to add; but to prepare themselves for even greater productivity upon their return.

□

44
Mr. Maurice and Telephones

Let's start with the basics: Mr. Maurice would like very much to uninvent the telephone. Yes, if he had a time machine (he's working on it!), he would zip back to the era of Alexander Graham Bell and whisper a few words of warning in his ear. Surely, Mr. Bell had no idea what havoc for the future he was creating. With Mr. Maurice's cautions in mind, Bell would surely follow a different course – and with no regular old-time telephones to build upon, the dreaded cell phone and its latest offshoots might never have developed at all.

Why is Mr. Maurice so down on cell phones – and phones of every stripe? Mainly, in addition to their being so ever-present as to annoy, they make personal communication too easy, and thereby too trivial.

Who are they all talking to, Mr. Maurice inquires frequently, but no useful answer has been forthcoming. Why are they talking so much? No reasonable response to that one, either. Maurice simply cannot fathom that more than a teeny-tiny percentage of the calls made at any given moment are of any importance whatsoever, much less urgent.

Cell-phone and landline users alike might choose to differ, but in Maurice's view, calls are too darned cheap. They're also too quick, too efficient, too simple to enact.

As a result, they've distorted the very nature of personal communication.

Now, admirers of Mr. Maurice might be surprised to hear him deplore efficiency in any way. Ordinarily, he would agree that efficiency is good. But not on the phone. Maurice actually longs for the days when a long-distance call – or better yet, an international one – was a special event, an occasion, a time-consuming ritual that made the result seem important. How important is a call today, which can be completed in seconds – even when phoning to the other side of the world?

In some parts of the world, Maurice points out, phoning is still like it used to be. In areas of Mexico, for instance, while cell phones are almost as ubiquitous as they are in the United States, Canada, and Europe, folks who lack a "cell" can trot down to a storefront telephone office. Just as they might have 30 or 40 years ago, they can pay for calls at so-many pesos per minute.

Then again, it's not quite the same as it used to be. Years back, callers had to give the desired phone number to an operator, then take a seat while she attempted to make the call – and often failed, through several attempts. If she succeeded, you'd step into a phone booth (yes, the old-fashioned enclosed kind) and start talking. Afterward, you paid by the minute. If failure persisted, you'd be told to come back tomorrow. Today, you can usually dial the number yourself, and it's far more likely to go through – but that call still seems a lot more important for having gone through the routine of going to a special place to make it. Maurice gives the old-fashioned way a big hooves-up.

45

Mr. Maurice and Advertising

"Eek! Eek!" Mr. Maurice oinks with unbridled derision whenever he encounters a TV commercial. Not because he would like to purchase the proffered product or service, but because he is offended by the notion of someone attempting to induce him to buy it. All the more so when trickery, deceit, and gimmickry take the place of useful information – which is how most commercials are prepared these days, in Maurice's view.

No punches are pulled when Mr. Maurice ponders the world of advertising, whether on TV, in print, on billboards, or anywhere else. All four of his hooves are pointed downward in a stinging rebuke of the whole idea of advertising.

That advertising has become the preferred method for swaying voters toward a candidate is, in Maurice's esteemed opinion, appalling. He is especially incensed – indeed, livid – by the prevalence of venomous and hateful negative ads, typically loaded with lies and false innuendoes, that clutter the airwaves in every political campaign season.

"After all the debates and discussions on TV and in the papers," Maurice notes, "voters still make their choices based on commercials?" Tossing his head back and sending his hoofs into the air, Mr. Maurice is so repelled that he cannot even bring himself to laugh at this absurdity.

□

46

Mr. Maurice and the Law

In theory, according to Mr. Maurice's analysis, the law is a thing of absolute, great beauty, comparable to a vivid rural landscape or the flow of a woman's breast. In reality, he adds hastily, the law can be a dunce, a mishmash, a glaring example of sheer horror. Results emanating from far too many courts qualify as little more than a hodgepodge of nonsense and foolishness that delivers the wrong solution far more often than it should. That's Maurice's educated perspective, after his ambitious and tenacious study of the legal system as it's promised, and as it works in the real world.

"The law is an ass." Mr. Maurice would not go quite that far in his ridicule, echoing this statement that dates back to the early seventeenth century. Popularized by Charles Dickens, who has Mr. Bumble, a character in *Oliver Twist*, state it emphatically when questioning a legal decision, the comment refers to an obstinate donkey; but it often is used to characterize the stupid rigidity of many legal actions.

Maurice reserves special derision for the jury system: elegant in theory, but falling far short in reality. Following a lengthy trial controlled by a rigorous set of rules, the jury retires to the jury room and debates upon a verdict with no rules at all! Mr. Maurice cannot understand why hardly anyone other than himself finds this practice to be strange and dangerous. He calls it the "second trial."

As for the "first" trial, he still has trouble believing that prosecutors and defense attorneys both aim to "win" rather than to achieve justice. Even though Maurice is capable of arguing for hours nonstop, he winced when he learned that one of his favorite lawyers of the past, Clarence Darrow, once demanded that he be permitted to speak for a matter of days in his zeal to defend a client. That both sides of a dispute can make believable claims to be right is a dilemma that makes Mr. Maurice's oversize head hurt.

That's just the beginning of Maurice's ferocity about the legal system, which puts expediency above truth, relies upon impartiality that does not exist, is built upon the presumption of innocence that many juries ignore, and issues prison sentences that vary with the defendant's race, class, and quantity of assets. Maurice is one of the group who views prisons as essentially schools for crime, packed with unfortunate folks who committed relatively trivial offenses.

Don't even ask what he thinks about the current Supreme Court.

Maurice likes the idea of punishment; though not, of course, if he's on the receiving end. If everyone did their duty and followed rules, he notes, there would be no need for laws. Pigs know that.

As for the police, Mr. Maurice likes to recall the words of a surly Marlon Brando in his role as Johnny, the head of the Black Rebels Motorcycle Club, in the 1953 film *The Wild One*. "I don't like cops," Brando reports with a suitable sneer.

Contracts? In Maurice's world, a firm hoofshake is far more important than any words on paper. Unlike humans, a pig's word is always good.

□

47

Mr. Maurice and Violence

How could they? Whether individually, in groups, by country or region, how could anyone knowingly and intentionally inflict pain and suffering upon a fellow creature? That's what Mr. Maurice would like to know, but don't bother to try and explain because he knows there is no valid answer to that question. There cannot, and will not, be any justification – ever – for inflicting violence upon each other without regard for even the most elemental levels of decency. Not as long as Mr. Maurice is in charge.

Ah, yes, it's true that Mr. Maurice is not actually in charge. Not yet, at any rate. But if he were, you can bet that he would put an end to all the violent acts that take place. He hasn't specified exactly how that would happen, but everyone acquainted with Maurice knows that if anyone can do it, that would be him.

If anything at all makes Mr. Maurice cringe, that would be violence.

Now, Mr. Maurice is of course the most decent and gentle of creatures himself, and cannot possibly conceive of harming anyone in any way. Except, perhaps, by inducing one of his many underlings to work harder and harder, to the point of exhaustion, in order to replenish Mr. Maurice's personal coffers and maintain his ever-growing shopping list.

While clearly incapable of causing any harm himself, Mr. Maurice does admit that the right to defend oneself and one's family from the aggressive, barbaric behavior of lesser creatures can on occasion warrant raising a hand – or a hoof – to fend off one's attacker. Or, even to strike a blow for civility on an even rarer occasion. Evidence exists that Maurice has indeed done so himself on more than one occasion, but don't try to get him to talk about it. He would rather bite you than admit to participation in a physical altercation.

☐

48

Mr. Maurice and Traffic

Although Mr. Maurice lacks a state-issued driving license, and has never officially learned to operate an automobile, he has some strong opinions on cars.

Mr. Maurice Knows It All ... and tells you so

Not everyone knows this, but Maurice occasionally does slip behind the wheel, license or not. Actually, he loves to drive. Because he resides in the household of an automotive journalist, at least one new car is likely to be in the apartment complex's parking lot, loaned out by the manufacturer for evaluation purposes.

Though Mr. Maurice normally shuns the ordinary Hondas and Toyotas, and fails even to glance at subcompact economy cars, availability of a luxury model – or a mammoth SUV – is quite another story. He is definitely not above surreptitiously grabbing the keys so he can take a spin around the neighborhood – or even farther afield – to show off and revel in posh motoring.

When the vehicle at hand for a week is a BMW, Mercedes-Benz, Lexus, Jaguar, or Cadillac, you can be sure that Mr. Maurice will take the wheel at least once. Maurice is especially fond of convertibles, since having the top down gives onlookers a chance to ogle his magnificent countenance as he glides by.

Most of his driving is done at night, however, so he doesn't draw excess attention either from the authorities or from his many admirers. No one seems to know how his short little hoofed legs manage to reach the pedals, or how his short arms can manipulate the steering wheel most effectively. But he invariably brings the car back without a scratch, so obviously he has found a way to make it happen. Anyone who has seen his current conveyance roll by, Maurice's jaunty black beret barely visible above the seat, knows that he is an avid little motorist.

☐

49

Mr. Maurice and Patience

On the surface, Maurice comes across as an amazingly patient pig. Nothing seems to faze him. If someone is slow to react, delivers an annoying message, or dawdles in his or her duties, Maurice displays not a particle of impatience with that offender.

Underneath, on the other hand, he is almost invariably seething. His hooves, were they brought into view, are surely clenched, and often tap-tapping on the floor. His snout's nostrils are tight, while his mouth bears the beginnings of a grimace. In short, despite outward appearances and manifestations, Maurice is about ready to explode. Clearly, he is in need of some deep breaths to restore calm to his psyche.

Everyone is in such a hurry these days, Maurice often laments. Why? Where are they going? That's what Mr. Maurice would like to know. Most important, why aren't they all at work where they belong (see section on Traffic, above), making money that might eventually wind up inside Maurice's pocketbook.

Only one phenomenon causes Mr. Maurice to break his rule and exhibit patience. When his personal wishes are ignored by an underling, Maurice is sure to start growling and oinking with increasing frequency until the offender reestablishes the proper equilibrium and accedes to each of Maurice's desires.

50

Mr. Maurice and Conformity

Only if everyone in the world – or the universe – chose to conform to Mr. Maurice in thought and deed would he endorse conformity. That would, of course, be an utterly ideal state of affairs, so long as no one was so foolish as to believe they were actually becoming "like" Mr. Maurice in any conceivable way.

But no, even that would be a step in the wrong direction, Maurice realizes. Conformity to outside pressures, even a force as intense as his own, is never a good idea.

Maurice asks, though, what conformity actually means. In dress? In personal details? In behavior? In attitude (a term so overused nowadays that it makes Mr. Maurice cringe)?

What about young folks with multiple earrings, piercings both seen and unseen, tattoos in growing number – like millions of others roaming today's streets and, frankly, sitting in today's office suites. How different are they from the gray-flannel suits of conformist 1950s America, Maurice wonders. Or from the ripped jeans and tie-dyes that emerged during the counterculture era of the 1960s and 1970s – not to mention the long hair and beards that became a virtual badge of belief in those days.

Or even from the crew cuts that marked obedient young men in an earlier time.

Isn't it better if each of us stands back and says, "I'm going to be myself," whatever that entails. That's how Maurice counsels each member of his pig family, after all. Want a tattoo? Crave a tongue piercing? Then get one – but only if it truly pleases you, not your peers. Why should we care what they think? If they're only accepting us because we look and act like them, what's the point of having them as friends?

To illustrate, Mr. Maurice calls attention to the popular book and film *The Girl with the Dragon Tattoo*. Especially in the novel, the story starts slowly, almost boring. But as soon as Lisbeth arrives on the scene, as one of the least-conformist characters in recent fiction, the pace intensifies and she – piercings, sullenness and all – leaps into the story as the focal point. Why? Because despite appearance, she is good at what she does. Really good. Isn't that all that should matter?

If your personal peers look like tattered derelicts most of the time, but you're most comfortable in a suit and tie, don't even think about going their way. Buy the suit, and wear it proudly. Similarly, if your peer groups resembles the sedate Ivy Leaguers of a half-century ago, but you're a whiskery, bedraggled sort yourself, no real friend would expect you to change to suit the group.

For women, Maurice's recommendation differs not a whit. If your lady friends wear jeans and boots but you're pleased by short skirts and heels, or by shaded sheer stockings and sandals, go your own way. Pay no attention to their opinions. Do what's most satisfying to you, Maurice advises, and you'll never regret it in the end.

Mr. Maurice Knows It All ... and tells you so

□

51

Mr. Maurice and Interactivity

Even an inveterate TV watcher doesn't want to devote big chunks of time to the latest "news" about favorite shows. Yet, that's what marketers of sitcoms and dramatic shows want these days. They want viewers to interact with other "fans" to discuss the show and its characters online, to play games related to the show, to clamor for members-only clips of forthcoming episodes. It's simply the latest incarnation of "customer reviews" of everything, whereby consumers are encouraged to share their opinions on nearly every product or service they might use.

Peer-to-peer interaction. That's what they call it. That's not what Mr. Maurice calls it, however. He calls it hogwash. A total waste of time. Foolish nonsense. (Or occasionally by some cruder name, which shall not be conveyed in this chapter).

For one thing, Mr. Maurice has no peers. He is, as we've clearly seen, one unique pig. Therefore, why would he wish to interact – in person or electronically – with any of his lessers?

Being part of a community can be valuable, Maurice admits, even though his is largely a community of one: himself. But these online versions are communities of strangers. Punching keys and watching a screen isn't how anyone is supposed to interact with the world, he's certain. It's an illusion – and Mr. Maurice deplores illusions.

Peer-to-peer interaction is also a way to eliminate professional critics and analysts. Mr. Maurice points out with a powerful shaking of his hoof that it could even mean eliminating the perfect opinions emanating from himself! Obviously, this practice must be curtailed, and soon.

Though he won't always admit it, Maurice has on occasion been more interactive than his admirers might believe. He has, in fact, even tried computer dating a few times, when seeking a partner the old-fashioned way has proven to be ineffectual or overly slow.

As for the tendency to have everyone's opinion become equal on the Internet, thus negating the entire concept of expertise on a subject, Maurice turns wild at the very thought of it. He recalls a retort from author Fran Lebowitz, which was so perfect that he wishes he'd come up with it himself. Referring to web sites and TV programs that close by saying, "We want to know what you think," Ms. Lebowitz had a two-word answer: "I don't." For that brief reaction, Maurice frequently gives Ms. Lebowitz a four-hoofed salute.

□

52

Mr. Maurice and Privacy

Being an intensely private pig himself, Maurice is distressed by the invasion of 24/7 observers, made possible by fast and tiny electronic gadgetry. His precious London, where he was knitted, has earned the dubious record of being the most spied-upon city in the western world.

Countless cameras spy upon passersby all over that great historic metropolis. Each camera watches the daily life that passes before it, passing along all details to anonymous workers in some unknown location. Each citizen and visitor can expect to have his or her movements tracked all day long, no matter what they're doing, or where they're going. In Maurice's view, this dreadful scab upon the face of democracy is all too reminiscent of the spied-upon citizenry of the old Soviet Union, or China today.

That's but one of the intrusions we face daily, each of which turns Mr. Maurice's countenance red with ferocity. Tragically, many of the losses of privacy have come about voluntarily – mainly with the development and proliferation of the cell phone. Maurice has no such device at hand, and deplores their incessant use. In fact, he longs for the days of the enclosed phone booth (largely extinct before his time), when people preferred to keep their personal business to themselves and the single person being called.

Maurice does not wish to hear about your relationship with your wife, your boss, your paramour, your children, or anything else. Unless, of course, those bits of knowledge might benefit *him* in some way – preferably monetarily.

In addition to on-street cameras, we must face listening devices, Internet monitoring, e-mail scrutiny, opening of private mail. Now, GPS units in cars can inform authorities where we've been during the course of a day. In so many ways, we've lost our entire sense of privacy, Maurice laments. What's next? A GPS inside everyone's head?

As for invasion of privacy by scrutinizing your computer, coupled with keystroke analysis, Maurice himself has been known to gaze upon barely-clad beauties on his own computer screen, and to investigate financial details of cohorts whom he suspects of not turning over sufficient funds to him. He certainly does not want you or anyone else to know the details of those activities.

□

53

Mr. Maurice and Discrimination

Let's be frank about this: Mr. Maurice has suffered discrimination throughout his existence on the grounds that he is:

1. A pig, rather than a human.

2. Not alive, in the usual sense.

Naturally, he realizes that the slings and arrows aimed in his direction for the above reasons are as nothing compared to the persecutions experienced by black slaves, by today's "illegal" immigrants, by Jews in Nazi Germany. Still, being an empathetic pig, he believes he has at least an inkling of what those unfortunate groups faced.

Maurice, being a logical thinker and avid reader, thought that era was long gone. He is in fact flabbergasted that discrimination still persists – especially the kind based on race, but other types as well.

Maybe discriminatory thoughts cannot be controlled, but actions can. Maurice has read and seen films of the Civil Rights struggle, the suffragettes seeking the vote for women, strikes against bosses who relied on discrimination to keep the workers at odds with each other. Shocking as it is to report, Mr. Maurice may have been mistaken in that assumption.

He is particularly incensed about assaults on the role of women, who certainly fare better than in the past, but not nearly as well as they should. Don't even ask him about the anti-woman stances taken by some of the "values-driven" presidential candidates in 2012. Maurice just might bite, he gets so worked up by lunacy of this sort.

□

54

Mr. Maurice and Travel

On many a quiet night, Maurice dreams of darting away to exotic locales. Beaches with sand like velvet droplets, mountain vistas reaching serenely into the sky to provide stunning views of all that lies below. Luxury trains, like the old Orient Express. Maurice pictures himself chatting amiably with movie stars, famous authors, glitzy celebrities.

Maurice loves to meditate upon travel, imagining all the places he might visit – destinations where he would of course be greeted and welcomed as the distinguished visitor he would be. He even enjoys planning out fantastic and lengthy trips, typically with stops at four-star (preferably five) hotels. He envisions being picked up at the airport by a neatly-dressed chauffeur with cap and tie, then whisked away via limousine. No two-star hotels, grungy hostels, or basic B&Bs for him.

When the time comes to purchase a ticket or book a room (preferably suite), however, he surreptitiously consults his pocketbook, looks puzzled for a few moments, then zips it back up with a flourish. "No," he will announce with a stately smile and a sense of finality, "not this time. I believe I'm needed here by all the piggies."

And so it goes, until the next time he comes across a lavish travel brochure, or spies bikini-clad ladies reveling in luxury at an expansive resort, in a TV commercial. Then, the cycle begins again.

Because Maurice's first lieutenant and principal assistant – aptly named LG (Little Guy) for his smaller stature – does travel extensively, Maurice gets regular reports from the field, as it were. He insists it's the next best thing to being there, while costing him nothing and requiring no expenditure of energy trudging through airports, traversing crooked narrow streets in European metropolises, or making his way up a mountainside to get a look at some antiquity or other.

LG has stayed in countless high-end hostelries (plus a number of lesser establishments), so his reports are varied and comprehensive, packed with intricate details of each trip. For the most part, then, Maurice elects to remain in his own sty. After all, he knows everything there is to know about the world, already.

Many believe that Maurice does have the ability to transport himself elsewhere – and possibly to other times as well. He won't admit it, but judging by some of the stories he tells about historical figures and places, some of us think he does possess a time machine. How else could he know about a certain dictator's propensity to sneeze when making a frenzied speech (never quite caught on camera)? Unless he was there, Maurice would not know what Casanova's many lady friends actually thought about his prowess – especially when compared to that of Mr. Maurice himself.

When Maurice goes to Paris, then, he's not exactly there, it appears – but not exactly "not there" either. Called upon to explain, he just displays his trademark little grin that says, without words, "wouldn't you like to know?"

55

Mr. Maurice and Cleanliness

Sad to say, pigs do have a reputation for slovenliness. To no one's surprise, Mr. Maurice begs to differ. Nay, he *demands* to differ.

Pigs are particularly clean, he insists. And of course, he is personally the most well-laundered pig on the planet.

How he achieves this immaculate state despite his intense aversion to water and distaste for soap is a mystery to all. Yet, the results speak most admiringly for themselves. Why, he simply shines, he shimmers, his pelt glows a lustrous pink hue, reflecting tiny twinkles off the sun when he deigns to enter the outdoors on a bright day. His precisely-spaced teeth, too, should you be among the fortunate few permitted to gaze upon them, sparkle like tiny searchlights.

Maurice, after all, is one mighty handsome pig. And he knows it.

Still, he disagrees with those who claim that "cleanliness is next to godliness," or who go overboard in their dedication to keeping their physiques in an immaculate state. For Mr. Maurice, clean behavior is the kind that counts. Having a clean pelt is essentially a bonus.

Actually, he loves to utter the concise comment: "No sweat." No one is ever quite sure if he's advising listeners not to worry about the troubles and tasks they face, or if he's simply noting that he, Maurice, *never* perspires.

☐

56

Mr. Maurice and Ownership

Since he already is the boss of all he surveys, and no one – pig or person – has the courage to challenge his status, Mr. Maurice has little desire to possess things. He is perfectly content to reside in a rented apartment, for instance – so long as someone else is paying the rent.

As long as his resting spot is comfortable, that's all that matters to Mr. Maurice, regardless of who owns the actual position. What difference does it make whose name is on an ownership paper, Maurice asks. The point is to make use of and enjoy the home, the space, the product – whatever it is.

Some observers consider Maurice's non-ownership preference to be practically Neanderthal, in view of his well-known propensity to grab every dollar on which he can lay his hooves. Maurice sees no contradiction whatsoever, and is mystified by all the regular people – rich and poor alike – who covet all the goods they can possibly acquire. He's seen the scenes of madness on the TV news when a once-a-year sales comes up, or the latest gadget from Apple hits the stores. Get up in the middle of the night and stand in line so you can be among the first to own the newest whatever? No thanks, says Mr. Maurice. He's deeply into his regular beauty sleep at that time – not that he needs it, of course.

Maurice is admittedly one seriously greedy little pig, but an acquisitive creature? Not at all. His abode is remarkably free of extraneous goods. Maurice wishes to spend his days on thoughts and ideas, not on shopping and gathering.

With ownership comes responsibilities, too. Therefore, Mr. Maurice is even more doubtful about its desirability, and would rather take no chances.

He does not like to affix his signature to any document, to tell the truth. In fact, hardly anyone has ever *seen* his signature. They wonder, too, how he can hold a pen in his hoofs, but Maurice is far more adept than most of us at making peak use of his faculties.

☐

57

Mr. Maurice and Pests

Maurice simply cannot abide pests. Not just rodents and insects, either, but pesky people. And yes, pesky pigs, too.

No thanks, he says. While he would never heedlessly stomp a hoof on any living creature, no matter how small,

Mr. Maurice Knows It All ... and tells you so

Mr. Maurice is not above kicking aside an especially disturbing intruder.

Worst of all, in his view, is the behavioral pest, of whatever lineage and background. Maurice simply deplores annoyances. When engaged in personal activities, he does not wish to be bothered in any way whatsoever. Be warned: he is prepared to bite, letting his normally-hidden primeval nature take precedence over his usual civility. His impeccable teeth are seldom seen behind his gracefully shut lips – but when they are, watch out!

As for small creatures that turn up, Maurice communes with them all, but has been known to jump headlong into the air at the sight of a rat or a snake. Having done so, he is contrite and apologetic to the unfortunate new arrival – perhaps inviting the interloper into his pen for a spot of tea to help smooth the waters.

□

58

Mr. Maurice and Charm

When you're overloaded with charm, how can you assess its value? Maurice will try.

Oh, he's a charmer, all right. A mere glance from his enthusiastic eyes has been known to induce certain females – whether person or pig – to squirm in delight at the thought of his amorous intentions. More than one has even begun to shed articles of clothing in anticipation, just in case Mr. Maurice is in the mood for dalliance, and even for romance, at that particular moment.

Well, that's the lurid story that surrounds his presence. Naturally, Mr. Maurice is too gallant to affirm the truth of such assertions.

Gentlemen, too, fall easily under the spell of Mr. Maurice's charming ways, impressed by his avid glance, his intelligent little smile, his knowing nod. Their reasons for being smitten by Mr. Maurice may differ, but the intensity of their response is a familiar one to him.

Being a charmer himself, he might either like or mistrust other charming folks. Maurice actually adores them, and whenever possible, he steers clear of those who *lack* charm. He's especially wary of – even antagonistic to – those who make no attempt to amass even a tiny bit of charm, or appear unaware that such a trait even exists. Sadly, there are so many of the uncharming among us.

So, can he actually "charm the pants off" a person? Well, not literally. Maurice would never use his personal attributes, his persuasive powers, for such a risque purpose. Not often, anyway, though he's frequently tempted. When you've "got it," and you know it, Mr. Maurice has been heard to admit, it's difficult to keep from making use of those benefits to your own advantage, even in the romance department. Sad to say, once in a great while, even the discreet and gentle Mr. Maurice can turn into a shameless cad.

☐

59

Mr. Maurice and Bad Behavior

So many of life's lessons may be learned from movies. Mr. Maurice has learned plenty since he came to America and became a devotee of films. He's especially taken with those that convey a message, which in his mind means most of them. Needless to say, he does not concur with the late movie producer Mr. Samuel Goldwyn, who said of films: "If you want to send a message, use Western Union." (Actually, when he first heard that quote, Maurice had to consult an encyclopedia to find out what Western Union was, as telegrams were before his time.)

Maurice often mentions the character played by Ben Johnson in *The Last Picture Show*, where he laments the "trashy behavior" that had become the rule even in his small Texas town. And that film was depicting the 1970s. Today, bad behavior has become so rampant that Mr. Maurice often says he'd like to stick his head in the sand and stay there, so he wouldn't have to see and hear any more trash talk and comparable behavior.

Officially, then, Maurice deplores bad behavior wherever and whenever it appears. Furthermore, he is dismayed by the phenomenon of young ladies expressing a preference for "bad boys" over "nice guys." He is even more incensed by young men speaking of their girlfriends – or ladies passing by – in gutter language. Why, he can't even bring himself to repeat some of the words he hears on the street. When passing a group of young fellows, he often wishes he had a cane at hand, so he could wallop each of them on the head after every barbarous utterance.

Also guaranteed to set him to oinking are young men calling their high-performance cars – or their guns – "bad boys," while boasting of their capabilities.

As for "bad girls," Maurice's tone changes just a bit. Those particular young ladies seem to revel in behaviors that, to be honest, Mr. Maurice finds rather enticing. Even erotic. He knows he should be ashamed of such thoughts, and that they might deserve a wallop from his nonexistent cane, too. He should be feeling guilty (see section 10). Yet, he is drawn to these young ladies with their split skirts, garish piercings, revealing blouses (with or without a bra beneath), their skintight jeans – and even by their unruly, defiant behavior.

When in a particularly relaxed mood, Mr. Maurice just might admit to being something of a "bad boy" himself. Or, in his case, a "bad pig." He does, after all, like to defy authority, to thumb his snout at convention.

Still, he knows that behaving properly is simply the right thing to do. But sadly, those temptations toward badness can be awfully hard to resist.

□

60

Mr. Maurice and Generosity

Maurice can be counted on to give a coin to a homeless

person, to provide a meal for one who's hungry – even if it means digging rather deeply into his sacrosanct pocketbook. This is an amazing phenomenon, because in all other respects, he is so defiantly miserly that dragging a penny out of his grasping hoof seems an impossible task. But he feels good when helping out a less-fortunate soul, and Maurice does like to feel good, however that's achieved.

Give until it hurts? Well, no, Maurice prefers to halt well before that point. Obviously, he will not cut too deeply into his collections of coins, much less of bills. Nevertheless, he does qualify as a generous pig.

What Maurice deplores is begging. Not so much by a down-and-out individual on the street. That just makes him sad and morose, and he declares that such a thing should not happen in a civilized world. No, what he truly detests is begging by big organizations, no matter how worthy their cause may be. Maurice considers these actions demeaning.

Twice a year, for instance, he becomes livid when some of his favorite PBS programs are interrupted for fund-raising. "Sure, they need funds," Maurice acknowledges. "But people should be giving because it's the right thing to do, not to get some little prize." Needless to say, he turns off the sound when the plea for donations begins, and sits, almost seething, until it ends.

□

61

Mr. Maurice and Courtesy

No pig or person could be more courteous, or more courtly, than Mr. Maurice. He simply does not countenance rudeness, and demands politeness from everyone around him.

With Mr. Maurice in the area, you can expect gallant behavior all-around, reminiscent of a far earlier, way more genteel era. Maurice could fit neatly into the formal court of a French or English king of the distant past – provided that he was granted an appropriately high title, that is. "'Sir Maurice' rolls off the tongue easily," he's been known to proclaim. That one has always appealed to him, perhaps because of his own British background.

Failing such a step back in time, Maurice enjoys exhibiting simple, basic courtesies in his daily life – especially when all around him are flaunting their rudeness and me-first behavior. Well, if anyone deserves to be "first," that would be Mr. Maurice, as any reasonable person will acknowledge.

Regardless, everyone he encounters can expect a gracious smile, an enthusiastic handshake (or hoofshake, as the case may be), a courtly bow at times – plus an overall aura of gentlemanliness that's seldom observed anymore. A bewitching greeting and a graceful adieu are part of Mr. Maurice's repertoire of civilized behavior. He wishes to be a powerful role model in this realm, to try and offset the crudity that has become part of modern life.

Never, ever, for example, would an off-color story or a crude word leave the lips of Mr. Maurice, particularly if a lady is present anywhere nearby. In fact, if he happens to hear you uttering such a comment, you can expect some harsh tongue-lashing or worse from one angry little pig.

☐

62
Mr. Maurice and Ethics

If any branch of philosophy scores Number One with Mr. Maurice, that would be Ethics. Despite his well-deserved reputation for greed and avarice, not to mention highly conspicuous consumption, Maurice is a supremely ethical pig.

Honesty, truth, integrity, too. These are the elements that make for an admirable life, in the mind of Mr. Maurice. It's all a matter of doing what's right, as they say, even when no one is looking. Well, Mr. Maurice is *always* looking, so the unethical had better be worried if they see him coming or hear his angry oinks drawing nearer.

Ethics matters two ways, Maurice explains: in business, and in our personal, private lives. Many examples can be brought to mind of prominent persons who exhibited highly ethical behavior in one element of their lives, but shabby, trashy, unethical antics in the other. Still, Maurice is certain that the two go together, and we should all strive to be as ethical as we can in *all* of our relationships with others.

That's what *he* does, of course. Even though he's a greedy, grasping little pig who's always clamoring for more bucks, every last one of his endeavors in the acquisitive realm is done with ethics uppermost. Mr. Maurice enjoys his voluminous financial rewards not because of any untoward behavior, but because he's simply so wise and knowledgeable. When you really are the smartest guy (or pig) in the room, or in the world, what other result could there be?

Can ethical behavior be taught? Maurice has a quick and valid answer to that one: Bernie Madoff. Maurice practically fell off his chair when he learned that Mr. Madoff had been teaching a class at a prominent university on – get this – Business Ethics. Yes, one of the biggest schemers in history was in the classroom, instructing fragile young minds on how to be ethical in their business dealings after graduation. Case closed, Maurice says. Either you have it, or you don't.

□

63

Mr. Maurice and Trust

When Maurice hears anyone respond to a situation with the two words, "Trust me," he cringes visibly and oinks nastily. He believes that's practically an invitation to avoid trusting that person with anything: a veritable guarantee of mistrust.

"Trust everyone, but cut the cards." Journalist Finley Peter Dunne came up with that axiom, and it's become Mr. Maurice's motto in the trust area. While he always assumes that everyone he deals with can be trusted – and he himself is the most trustworthy of them all – you can't be too careful. Especially when money is concerned.

If Maurice gives his word that he will do something for you, consider it practically done already. He is one pig who will not let you down. When help is needed, he is the one who can be counted on – so long as he is not required to open his pocketbook in the process.

Maurice is trustworthy with everything except, possibly, money. Sometimes, he just cannot help himself when entrusted with someone else's funds. On those distressing occasions, he finds himself "borrowing" a bit to take care of his latest shopping excursion. Maurice deeply regrets these lapses, and invariably promises to do better next time. Since excess shopping is his only vice, friends and colleagues do forgive him for this one element of misconduct.

□

64

Mr. Maurice and Time

As an ardent fan of Mr. Stephen Hawking, the severely-afflicted British scientist who's made a lifelong study of time and related matters, Mr. Maurice thinks a great deal about time. The passing of time. Past time. Future time. Or, as Mr. William Saroyan put in the title of his foremost play, *The Time of Your Life*.

More than most of us, Mr. Maurice is only too aware of how fleeting time is, and how rapidly it's passing by, little-noticed.

Simply put, there's never enough. No day is long enough for Maurice, who has so many colleagues to contact, friends to visit, places to see, ideas to hear. Even he has discovered no way to stretch time, even by a little. Instead, he concentrates on making every moment count. "Live each day as if it were your last," he often intones, echoing the words of the fictional H.H. "Breaker" Morant.

Punctuality, on the other hand, is not Maurice's preference, doubtless attributable to his European upbringing. When you have an appointment with Mr. Maurice, you can count on one thing: he will be late. Possibly, quite tardy indeed. But take heart; he will be there eventually, and it will have been well worth the wait.

☐

65

Mr. Maurice and Fashion

Oh, does Mr. Maurice ever love to watch those fashion

models on TV. Not just because they're so lovely, but because he wants to stay abreast of all the latest trends from France, Italy – all the hot spots of the world.

Odd, because Maurice rarely – if ever – changes his own outfit. True, his boldly black-and-white striped shirt and mysterious black beret convey an uncanny fashion sense, setting off his internal handsomeness. Most of his piggie family, of course, wear nothing at all, since they are, after all, pigs, not people. So, it's a bewildering mystery why he, Maurice, is so taken with fashion.

He can rattle off the big names as easily as someone else might recount the names of fast-food joints in their neighborhood. Prada, Louis Vuitton, Christian Dior. Van Heusen, Levi Strauss. If he chose to change his attire regularly, and had full access to their wares, just imagine what a shimmering fashion plate he might be, nodding and waving to admirers on his leisurely, daily strolls through the neighborhood.

Friends and cohorts are not quite sure if he has a closetful of identical shirts, or is really adept at laundering and drying the one. Because he is rarely, if ever, seen without his beret, and it's invariably sitting at the most dramatic angle, they even wonder if it's somehow attached to his head.

For someone who has the exact same wardrobe each and every day, Mr. Maurice is a fashion plate *extraordinaire*. For an extra bit of flair, his neck is invariably accented by a dashing red scarf. He always looks sharp, cool, well-tailored, in full control of all he surveys. Onlookers are barely aware that he wears no pants; that's how good he is at making the most of what he *does* have on.

66

Mr. Maurice and "isms"

Communism, socialism, libertarianism, vegetarianism. "Why so many 'isms' in America," Maurice asks. "And why are people so frightened of them? Sometimes, they even seem afraid to say the words, as if something nasty might rub off on them."

Having studied every sort of political treatise and movement from Karl Marx, Lenin, and Mao Tse-Tung on the one hand to Hitler, Mussolini, and sundry third-world dictators on the other, Maurice can only scratch his snout in dismay. He's read Ayn Rand, John Maynard Keynes, Christopher Hitchens, Milton Friedman, Paul Krugman, William F. Buckley, Christopher Lasch. All he wound up with were sore eyes.

At the end, all Maurice can do is recall the line referring to Lenin and Marx: "That's John Lennon and Groucho Marx." Maurice cannot recall the name of the comedian who came up with that one, but he was surprised to learn that the two men – despite a considerable age difference – shared many opinions.

Maurice couldn't believe it when venomous opponents of all of President Obama's policies tried to brand him as a socialist. "What are they talking about?" he asked during every evening newscast. "He's no more a socialist than that shrill Ms. Sarah Palin is."

Because Maurice has read his history and political science, he knows what socialism is – unlike most members of the voting public, he notes with a sense of disdain. However, that history also has shown him how charges of "socialist" and "communist" have been leveled at countless political figures over the past century. Clearly, in Maurice's appraisal, most of them were folks simply trying to do the right thing, one way or another; and for that they endured ceaseless name-calling, and worse.

"Communists are the past," Maurice warns with a note of exasperation. "Get over it."

☐

67

Mr. Maurice and Security

Even though he rarely flies, Mr. Maurice is a vigorous opponent of the TSA agents who fill the nation's airports. While he heartily endorses efforts to help keep passengers safe, he is utterly unconvinced that the TSA accomplishes any of that. Instead, he asserts, they wield total power at the security lanes, essentially terrorizing the hapless, harmless fliers who ease through the portal into the frightful invasive body-scanner. Or, at least as bad, into the arms of an agent ready to conduct a full body search.

Meanwhile, luggage is taken over to a counter where the agent will thumb through one's personal belongings and subject some of them to tests for explosives. Well,

Mr. Maurice is not happy to have his delicate personal goods ogled and fondled, much less be treated as a common criminal and made to walk through a nefarious scanning machine. "Why, they can see inside my pelt," he's complained.

While all this is happening to ordinary people, Maurice is convinced that actual terrorists – those who intend to commit mayhem aboard a plane – are permitted to slip through, undetected.

Obviously, those in charge think otherwise. But in Mr. Maurice's view, it's all an act, a charade, creating the illusion – but not the reality – of safety in the air. This happens because those in charge believe terrorists – or any bad guys – are stupid, and unable to learn from their errors of the past. They are not.

Being a wholly logical pig who uses reason to come up with solutions, Maurice endorses real, serious anti-terrorist measures. Government authorities should be concentrating on people who present a real danger. More important, they should be spending most of their time determining why terrorists behave as they do, and what can be done to curtail their efforts. Mr. Maurice does not back "pretend" activities that irritate and frustrate passengers while delivering no real security from global dangers.

Mr. Maurice also wishes those in power would do more to ensure the *personal* security, economic and otherwise, of Americans. No one should face the threat of homelessness, hunger, untreated disease and distress. "Where's that safety net they keep talking about?" he inquires frequently. "That's the kind of security needed most," he says, by piggies as well as persons.

Mr. Maurice oinks profuse apologies for becoming so serious on this particular issue. We all know that he does get carried away when certain topics come to the forefront.

□

68

Mr. Maurice and the Occupiers

"Well, it's about time," Maurice remarked when news of the Occupy Wall Street movement first appeared on his TV screen in the autumn of 2011. In fact, he breathed a heavy sigh of relief, calling out "At last" more than once. "Finally," he added, "the ordinary folks are waking up."

Now, several years after the movement began, Maurice is not so sure. Their points of concern are just as important as before, if not more so. Yet, he's been observing signs of deterioration into dissension and factionalism, like most protests of the past.

"Stay focused," he sometimes cries out at ears that pay no heed, when he happens to come across one of the remaining outposts of the Occupy movement. They are on the correct path, he believes; but detours appear to be popping up everywhere.

Still, he admires their determination. Their hardiness, their willingness to endure hardship – even beatings and jail – to further the advance of the "99 Percent." Greedy as he is, Maurice would never want to be thought of as fitting into the One Percenters, many of whom he considers villainous barbarians and – borrowing a term from the past – despicable "robber barons."

Although Maurice would certainly like to rank among the top 1 percent himself in terms of wealth, he is far from approving of their attitudes and behavior. Exceptions exist, he admits; but for the most part, he sees their greediness as damaging to the country and the world. Unlike Mr. Maurice's own avariciousness, that is, which is benign and beneficial to everyone. So, he wishes the Occupiers well and, should their activities be revived, advises that they might see him out on the barricades himself one of these days – perhaps holding a sign with a particularly pithy and pointed message that cannot be ignored.

☐

69

Mr. Maurice and Business

Long ago, in the early 1920s, then-President Calvin Coolidge uttered some notable words. "The business of America is business," he proclaimed.

Mr. Maurice could hardly disagree more. If business is put in its place, Maurice is okay with that. But he winces at the thought that it should be Number One on the national priority list.

Mr. Maurice Knows It All ... and tells you so

Oh, business is essential, Maurice admits. In Coolidge's day, businessmen were like the one depicted in Mr. Sinclair Lewis's great novel, *Babbitt* – narrow-minded but well-meaning. "Those days are gone," Maurice laments. If only today's businesspersons behaved in an admirable, conscientious way, accepting reasonable profits for their efforts, Maurice would have no problem with them.

When he hears about businesses that push the laws and the rules to squeeze out every last cent of profit, ignoring the impact of their misdeeds upon customers or clients, Mr. Maurice is ready to bring his twin whips into action. Businesspersons be warned: If you've been behaving improperly in the financial department and, one day, you see a little pink creature with a black beret striding down the aisle toward your office, you're in for a highly unpleasant surprise.

Personally, Maurice has any number of *little* businesses operating, though details are largely unknown. Evidently, they're so little that hardly anyone seems to know they exist. That's how Mr. Maurice likes it. If a business is too big, Maurice cannot be in full charge.

A few years back, when there was all this talk about businesses like General Motors being "too big to fail," Maurice took exception. If they're too big to fail, he warned, they're too big to exist in the first place.

Maurice has a particular aversion to the folks he calls money-changers and money-shufflers, mostly out of principle but also because they might impair the value of his own pocketbook with their wicked acts. The shuffling might take place electronically these days, but the result hasn't changed.

He also cannot stand middlemen, who reap in plenty of profits after contributing so little. But he reserves his harshest judgment for those in the insurance business. "Parasites of the earth," he screams when he hears about someone being rejected for health coverage because they might one day have to enter a hospital. Maurice is by no means alone in that appraisal of the insurance "profession" – a term that makes him snort and snarl.

Didn't Jesus Christ warn that money-changers should be driven from the temple? And doesn't the Bible advise that it's easier for a camel to fit through the eye of a needle than for a rich man to enter Heaven? Why have people forgotten these obvious truisms, Maurice wonders.

☐

70

Mr. Maurice and Salesmanship

"Now let's see," Maurice replied when told the nature of this chapter. "Salesmanship amounts to using manipulation and coercion to encourage someone to purchase your product," does it not?

Informed that it does, in essence, Mr. Maurice's personal response was a crude, noisy screech emanating from nearly-closed lips – what was once known as a "Bronx cheer." Clearly, he is not a fan of the business world.

Nobody likes compulsion and pressure, Maurice explained, except for the one who's wielding both. Why should anyone be encouraged to purchase what isn't wanted and isn't needed? Frankly, many salespeople qualify as parasites in the overall scheme of things – harsh words from Mr. Maurice, but true. Don't even get him started on the horrors of public relations (PR) people and how marketing has taken over the business world.

Maurice has read up on the history of salesmanship, both fictional and in the real world. On the positive side, he quotes from an old how-to tome by super-salesman Frank Bettger, titled *How I Raised Myself from Failure to Success in Selling*. He's seen the documentary film on door-to-door bible salesmen, and cannot fathom how anyone could be so callous as to prey upon grieving widows in order to make a few dollars. Now, he loves his dollars more than almost anyone short of Donald Trump and Bernie Madoff, but not when they're made by bilking people.

Willy Loman, the hapless old-time "drummer" in Arthur Miller's play *Death of a Salesman*, is Maurice's prime example of the horrors of a sales-oriented society. Just short of retirement age, Willy is fired by the company he's served for decades, selling "on the road." Maurice points out that in real life, that's been happening to plenty of employees as they reach their Sixties.

Maurice also looks to the past for the worst examples. Years ago, he learned, a furnace company established a model for deception. Their agents would use any subterfuge to get into a house, offering to inspect the owner's furnace. An hour or so later, the owner would come downstairs to check and discover that the old furnace was sitting in pieces on the floor. "Furnace is shot," the agent would lament – immediately offering to provide a spanking new unit for an outlandish price.

Online selling doesn't please Mr. Maurice, either. He doesn't often use the computer, but when he does, he invariably shrieks and oinks in disgust. "What are all these pop-up sales pitches," he asks. "And practically all these e-mails are trying to sell me something." Be warned: he's trying hard to think of a way to eradicate these electronic sales techniques, so that each of his e-mails will be from a friend or colleague, not somebody pushing questionable and unwanted goods.

Naturally, Maurice himself could sell anything to anyone, including the proverbial refrigerator to an Eskimo. But he would never accept such a role, regardless of how much it paid. Oh, wait, he's just tapped me on the shoulder to say there might be a limit to that last statement. Could this mean that, he, Maurice could conceivably be "bought?"

□

71

Mr. Maurice and Slimness

Not many of his friends and admirers are likely to mention it, but Mr. Maurice has a bit of girth himself these days – a touch of chunkiness upon his otherwise magnificent physique.

Mr. Maurice Knows It All ... and tells you so

Maurice likes ladies with some "meat on their bones," as certain gentlemen used to say. Pigs, of course, are well known for having plenty of meat – but as a civilized and urbane creature, he would prefer to be a bit on the slim side. Without overdoing it, of course. A seriously slim pig would be no pig at all, he is likely to point out.

No diets for Mr. Maurice, though, even if he consumed food in the customary way. No exercise routines, either, in view of his notorious aversion to perspiration.

Since he does not "eat" in the familiar manner, it's far easier for Maurice to avoid fattening meals than it would be for a human – or a conventionally live porker, for that matter. He admits that, and empathizes with those who struggle to slim down and cannot keep it up.

Maurice also is distressed by the young ladies who shun all foods, certain that they already are fat, when a mere glance reveals that they are already skeletally slender. How can they not see themselves correctly, as others see them, Maurice wonders.

Actually, he knows the answer, as do most of us nowadays: the media. Maurice is not one to blame the media for every ill in society, like many politicians and pundits of late; but in this case, their contribution to making a super-slim female body the one and only desirable model cannot be denied or overlooked. When are we going to start encouraging young women to value their feminine curves, even if they start leaning a little toward the chunky side? Mr. Maurice has seen more than enough skinny women breezing by. Come on, overly-slim ladies: let's not disappoint him.

72
Mr. Maurice and Food

Even though Maurice does not eat, at least in the customary way, he loves food. He revels in sniffing it, gazing at it, thinking about it – even tasting it, if surreptitiously. The only thing he doesn't do is consume those foods. That would be difficult, considering that he has no innards.

Yet, he savors the wafting aromas, the visual elegance of the well-prepared plate, the textures of each ingredient, even the sounds emanating from the kitchen. Maurice enjoys gourmet meals, ordinary lunches, midnight snacks – just about anything edible, as much as any human.

"There's nothing like a pretty plate," Maurice says.

Like so many of us, Mr. Maurice has some "guilty pleasures" in the food line. He adores soups, for instance, but he's glad he doesn't actually eat them, as they tend to be so – well, messy, dribbling off one's spoon. Unlike so many people, who shun vegetables as if they were vermin, Mr. Maurice loves his green beans, his corn (on the cob or off), his zucchini. Seafood? Yes, sir! Shrimp, fish (red snapper is his favorite, prepared Veracruz style), succulent lobster drenched in butter. Good thing Mr. Maurice doesn't have to worry about cholesterol! Doubtless related to his French background, he's particularly fond of *escargot* (that's snails, to the rest of us).

Maurice realizes that live piggies are not the most dainty eaters, wallowing so often in the mud and who-knows-what as they do. He would rather not think about that aspect of his live relatives, but he definitely wishes to set a far better example himself, serving as a role model to be admired and emulated. Or so he hopes.

Now and then, Maurice is tempted to dip his snout into a particularly attractive dish and snort away, like the live pigs of his acquaintance. But he resists – at least when anybody is looking.

□

73

Mr. Maurice and Alcohol

Of an evening, Mr. Maurice does enjoy a "couple of drinks." Like the fictional British spy James Bond, he is constantly searching for the perfect martini.

Nevertheless, Maurice is dismayed when he observes drinking to excess; and worse yet, outright drunkenness. Maurice is of course opposed to excess in every form (other than the accumulation of dollars, for which he sees no finite limit). When he sees someone weaving around unsteadily, speaking in a slurred voice, behaving crudely, he wants to go and bop them on the head, to try and instill some decency and decorum.

He is even more adamant about the dangers of drug use, and cannot comprehend how young people elect to distort their still-growing minds with illicit chemicals. "Why would anyone choose to damage and disfigure their brains with drugs?" he often asks. Not to mention the risk of overdoses and frightful effects as a result of drug-taking. "The brain is all we have that matters," Maurice explains, shaking his head in a mix of anguish and fury at this particular brand of human stupidity.

Maurice does not consume alcohol at home, which would set a poor example for the younger, more vulnerable pigs. Neither does he dash out in the evening to "have a beer with the boys." He is most emphatically not a "shot and a beer" sort of pig.

No, he prefers the cool milieu of an elegant cocktail lounge, filled with attractive ladies and nattily-attired gentleman. Maurice favors the old-time drinks: not just martinis, but also Manhattans, vodka tonics, a fine Scotch, even a sweet Bacardi now and then. He's been known to partake of some top-end whiskies on occasion – the occasion being when someone else is buying. Maurice has been known to buy a round of drinks "for the house," but not often. Not at all. And never when the group at the bar contains more than three or four imbibers. "No point getting carried away with this 'buy a round' business," he proclaims when asked why he often disappears just when the bartender appears to request payment for the previous order.

What Maurice cannot abide are the silly, fancy drinks that have become popular of late, including a zillion varieties of martini. To him, there's only one kind: the right kind.

◻

74

Mr. Maurice and Languages

In view of his monumental mental capacity, it's no wonder that Mr. Maurice is fluent in every known language on earth. And possibly, several that emerged from elsewhere.

So easy for Maurice; so hard for most of us.

Maurice actually has the answer for this quandary. It's confidence. Because Mr. Maurice is supremely confident, he's always ready to wade into a conversation with anyone. Even if those words from a stranger are in a dialect he's never heard before, Mr. M's confidence roars through and he manages to communicate.

If only the non-linguistic among us could be so sure of ourselves.

Maurice simply does not hesitate to immerse himself in foreign tongues and foreignness, surrounding himself with natives whom he does not yet understand. Surprisingly soon, he will. No book or CD lessons for him; no grammatical exercises needed until *after* he's mastered the rudiments of speech and conversation.

Obviously, what Mr. Maurice can accomplish language-wise in mere moments would take the rest of us weeks, months, even years to achieve. And few of us would ever be quite as relaxed among foreign speakers as he is.

Because Maurice is a pig of the world, how could he not be a superior linguist? Besides, as an incurable gatherer of information about people – some envious folk, as we've seen, brand him a gossip – he absolutely must be conversant in every tongue that might be spoken in his presence, so that he doesn't miss anything.

□

75

Mr. Maurice and Worry

What, Mr. Maurice worry? He loves Alfred E. Newman, that old character on Mad Magazine covers, who regular stated: "What, Me Worry?"

Even though there's plenty to worry about in a world filled with dangers of every scope and sort, Maurice never lets himself be drawn into fretting even a little. This is one confident little pig!

At least, that's his goal, though reality keeps chiming in. Maurice invariably warns others not to worry, because it just doesn't pay off – and he knows his stuff about getting paid! Nevertheless, he can't always stop himself from fretting. After all, he explains, there's so much to worry about nowadays: his own pig family, young pigs coming up, aggressive behavior (mainly from humans), and the inevitable crime. Yes, he admits, even pigs can perpetrate hostile acts.

How can anyone not worry, he adds, about the threat of additional warfare instigated by the warmongers throughout the country and the world. Look at all the high-tech weapons they keep coming up with, having no purpose but to kill. Drones, so the killing can effectively take place a thousand miles away from the target. What about those demonic dictators scattered across the globe. Hostile, even hateful political candidates who want to tear away rights granted long ago to the people.

"Only a fool would not worry," he concludes. Why, it's a wonder that Mr. Maurice is able to smile about anything!

And yet, he does. If only more of us could follow his stunning example.

□

76

Mr. Maurice and the Wild Life

There's a wild little pig lurking inside Mr. Maurice. He knows it, and everyone around him knows it. Only occasionally do glimpses of that wildness appear to outsiders, and then only momentarily.

According to Maurice, a wild man, woman, or pig lurks inside *each* of us, just waiting to be released and unleashed. For most of us, that wildness never gets out. For many, it doesn't even begin to knock at the exit door. Unlike most, Mr. Maurice has learned to release his inner wildness in stages, carefully, without letting it get too far out of hand.

Liberating that inner wildness doesn't have to result in risk-taking or adventurous endeavors, he hastens to add. Maurice points out that many of those seemingly unrestrained undertakings that have grown so popular among affluent tourists aren't really as "wild" as they appear.

No, unchaining the inner being certainly doesn't require traveling to exotic locales, humiliating oneself, or behaving foolishly. Going wild is just a matter of reaching the point where you don't hold back because of what others think (or you believe them to think), or due to dubious rules of civilized behavior that promote control over imagination. It's a matter of overcoming – not succumbing to – lethargy and apathy.

Instead, Maurice explains, you find your own unique way to release your inner self: the one that truly matters. Contrary to what some people seem to believe, going wild has nothing to do with inflicting harm on anyone in any way, or with insulting or harassing anyone. That's phony wildness, typified by certain right-wing pundits and aggressive rock musicians.

No, we're talking about the real thing. After all, some of the wildest eruptions can emanate from those among us whom we take to be the least likely to "go wild."

□

77

Mr. Maurice and the Past

The past is gone. Simple as that. *Finis. Au revoir. Sayonara* and *adios*. Maurice concentrates on today and tomorrow, always assuming they will be even more marvelous than yesterday.

Naturally, because he finds so much wrong with the world around him at the present time, and seldom hesitates to say so (as we've seen in these pages), *either* the past or the future might be preferred.

Of course, if Maurice was not there when something happened, it doesn't really count anyway. Looking back at historical personages, he simply says: They came, some of them tried, most of them failed. Case closed. Let's think about today, which is still here, and beyond.

Still, he does admire some parts of the past. In pop music, for instance, he's especially fond of Billy Joel, Bonnie Raitt, Rickie Lee Jones. Classics, too. He gets almost teary when hearing a Liszt Prelude, Beethoven's Fifth Symphony, or Smetana's *Moldau*. Or, most notably, any Puccini opera – though his favorite is *Turandot*. Nothing is more stimulating to Maurice than the musical version of *Les Miserables*, especially its rousing, revolutionary call to the barricades. And as for movies, as we've already seen, he's a classic film buff *par excellence*.

But politics? Government? Economics? History generally? If those fellows from the past were so smart, Maurice asks, why do we still have wars, poverty, suffering, karaoke, and Rush Limbaugh?

78

Mr. Maurice and the Future

Well, what else *is* there?

When the past is gone, and the present fails to measure up to our hopes and expectations, all we can do is look ahead.

During the period when Mr. George W. Bush was in office, Mr. Maurice was morose. Being a supreme thinker himself, he could not understand how the people had put Mr. Bush, an obvious non-thinker, into such a lofty position. Subsequent events affirmed Maurice's early appraisal.

Because he is inevitably a liberal thinker, he cheered up considerably when Mr. Barack Obama won election. That elation did not last long. When Maurice heard members of the opposition party declare that their foremost goal was to beat Mr. Obama the next time around, and then take steps to oppose every one of his proposals, often unanimously, Maurice knew that the world had turned topsy-turvy. "This is like 'Alice in Wonderland,'" he was heard to say many times, or like Mr. George Orwell's *doublethink*. "Up is down, good is bad, war is peace."

Difficult as it is to believe, Mr. Maurice is essentially an incurable optimist – albeit with a cantankerous twist.

How could it be any worse than now, he often inquires. Poverty, hatred, brutality, hunger all over the planet. No chance of there being a job for everyone, or even a speck of food for everyone in the world. At the same time, the rich getting even richer – though he wouldn't mind adding further to his personal pocketbook, Mr. Maurice reminds us.

Even though Mr. Maurice realizes that the next batch of political leaders – the ones who preach fear and intolerance – might achieve power, he believes that something good might come of it all. Asked what that might be, he goes momentarily mute, to be sure – an unfamiliar response for a pig who is ordinarily so conversationally astute. Still, if Mr. Maurice believes the civilized world is not yet about to end, and hope remains despite all the strife and devastation taking place around the world, who are we to disagree with him?

About Mr. Maurice

Mr. Maurice at work in a hotel room, dictating his pointed, penetrating thoughts to the author. Both creatures – stuffed pig and human – do some of their best thinking in hotels, away from the distractions at their office, or in the apartment they share with the author's wife, Marianne. Though Mr. Maurice was born/knitted in London, England, by a pair of older ladies, his French heritage is evident.

About the Author

James M. Flammang has been a journalist, writer, and editor for his entire working life. Since the 1980s, he's covered the automobile business as an independent journalist. In addition to contributing countless product reviews and feature articles to such publications as autoMedia, Kelley Blue Book, New Car Test Drive, CarsDirect.com, J.D. Power, cars.com, Consumer Guide, and the *Chicago Tribune*, Flammang has authored more than two dozen books. Most of those titles were about automotive history, but he also has written six books for children. Flammang is a member of the Freelancers Union, as well as the International Motor Press Association and Midwest Automotive Media Association (past president).

During the past few years, Flammang has eased away from the automobile business in order to concentrate on books: mostly essays and memoirs, along with a bit of fiction. *Mr. Maurice....* is the first of those titles, to be followed by *Incompetent*, *Absurdities*, *Hotel Life*, and *Fraidy-Cat*. He is also working on buying guides for used cars and hybrid/electric automobiles. Born in Chicago, Flammang lives just outside that city with his wife, advisor and editor, Marianne (who also answers to the name, Petunia).

www.ingramcontent.com/pod-product-compliance
Lightning Source LLC
Chambersburg PA
CBHW070627300426
44113CB00010B/1691